My
Facebook®
for Seniors
FOURTH EDITION

W9-BUH-447

WITHDRAWN

Michael Miller

QUe®

My Facebook® for Seniors, Fourth Edition

Copyright © 2019 by Pearson Education, Inc.

AARP is a registered trademark.

No part of this publication may be reproduced, stored in a retrieval system, or transmitted in any form or by any means, electronic, mechanical, photocopying, recording, scanning, or otherwise, except as permitted under Section 107 or 108 of the 1976 United States Copyright Act, without the prior written permission of the Publisher. No patent liability is assumed with respect to the use of the information contained herein.

Limit of Liability/Disclaimer of Warranty: While the publisher, AARP, and the author have used their best efforts in preparing this book, they make no representations or warranties with respect to the accuracy or completeness of the contents of this book and specifically disclaim any implied warranties of merchantability or fitness for a particular purpose. No warranty may be created or extended by sales representatives or written sales materials. The advice and strategies contained herein may not be suitable for your situation. You should consult with a professional where appropriate. The publisher, AARP, and the author shall not be liable for any loss of profit or any other commercial damages, including but not limited to special, incidental, consequential, or other damages. The fact that an organization or website is referred to in this work as a citation and/or a potential source of further information does not mean that the publisher, AARP, and the author endorse the information the organization or website may provide or recommendations it may make. Further, readers should be aware that Internet websites listed in this work may have changed or disappeared between when this work was written and when it is read.

ISBN-13: 978-0-7897-6027-2
ISBN-10: 0-7897-6027-4

Library of Congress Control Number: 2018948908

Printed in the United States of America

01   18

Trademarks

All terms mentioned in this book that are known to be trademarks or service marks have been appropriately capitalized. Que Publishing cannot attest to the accuracy of this information. Use of a term in this book should not be regarded as affecting the validity of any trademark or service mark.

Warning and Disclaimer

Every effort has been made to make this book as complete and as accurate as possible, but no warranty or fitness is implied. The information provided is on an "as is" basis. The author, AARP, and the publisher shall have neither liability nor responsibility to any person or entity with respect to any loss or damages arising from the information contained in this book.

Special Sales

For information about buying this title in bulk quantities, or for special sales opportunities (which may include electronic versions; custom cover designs; and content particular to your business, training goals, marketing focus, or branding interests), please contact our corporate sales department at corpsales@pearsoned.com or (800) 382-3419.

For government sales inquiries, please contact governmentsales@pearsoned.com.

For questions about sales outside the U.S., please contact intlcs@pearsoned.com.

Editor-in-Chief
Brett Bartow

Executive Editor
Laura Norman

Marketing
Stephane Nakib

Director, AARP Books
Jodi Lipson

Editorial Services
The Wordsmithery LLC

Managing Editor
Sandra Schroeder

Senior Project Editor
Tonya Simpson

Indexer
Cheryl J. Lenser

Proofreader
Gill Editorial Services

Technical Editor
Jeri Usbay

Editorial Assistant
Cindy J. Teeters

Cover Designer
Chuti Prasertsith

Compositor
Bronkella Publishing, LLC

Contents at a Glance

Table of Contents

About the Author

Michael Miller is a prolific and popular writer of more than 200 nonfiction books who is known for his ability to explain complex topics to everyday readers. He writes about a variety of topics, including technology, business, and music. His best-selling books for Que include *My Windows 10 Computer for Seniors*, *My Social Media for Seniors*, *My Smart Home for Seniors*, *My Internet for Seniors*, *My Samsung Galaxy S7 for Seniors*, *Easy Computer Basics*, and *Computer Basics: Absolute Beginner's Guide*. Worldwide, his books have sold more than 1.5 million copies.

Find out more at the author's website: www.millerwriter.com

Follow the author on Twitter: molehillgroup

Dedication

To my grandkids, who make my life fun and meaningful—Collin, Alethia, Hayley, Jackson, Judah, and Lael.

Acknowledgments

Thanks to all the folks at Que who helped turned this manuscript into a book, including Laura Norman, Charlotte Kughen, Tonya Simpson, Tricia Bronkella, and technical editor Jeri Usbay. Thanks also to Jodi Lipson and the kind folks at AARP for adding even more to the project.

Note

Most of the individuals pictured throughout this book are of the author himself, as well as friends and relatives (and sometimes pets). Some names and personal information are fictitious.

About AARP

AARP is a nonprofit, nonpartisan organization, with a membership of nearly 38 million, that helps people turn their goals and dreams into *real possibilities™*, strengthens communities, and fights for the issues that matter most to families, such as healthcare, employment and income security, retirement planning, affordable utilities, and protection from financial abuse. Learn more at aarp.org.

We Want to Hear from You!

As the reader of this book, you are our most important critic and commentator. We value your opinion and want to know what we're doing right, what we could do better, what areas you'd like to see us publish in, and any other words of wisdom you're willing to pass our way.

We welcome your comments. You can email or write to let us know what you did or didn't like about this book—as well as what we can do to make our books better.

Please note that we cannot help you with technical problems related to the topic of this book.

When you write, please be sure to include this book's title and author as well as your name and email address. We will carefully review your comments and share them with the author and editors who worked on the book.

Email: feedback@quepublishing.com

Reader Services

Register your copy of *My Facebook for Seniors* at www.informit.com/aarp for convenient access to downloads, updates, and corrections as they become available. To start the registration process, go to quepublishing.com/register and log in or create an account.* Enter the product ISBN, 9780789760272, and click Submit. Once the process is complete, you will find any available bonus content under Registered Products.

*Be sure to check the box that you would like to hear from us in order to receive exclusive discounts on future editions of this product.

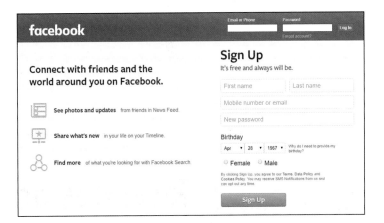

In this chapter, you find out how to create a new Facebook account and start using the Facebook website.

Getting to Know Facebook on Your Computer

Facebook has more than two billion members online, of all ages and types. Chances are your family and friends are already using Facebook—which means it's time for you to join in, too.

While almost all Facebook users access the service at one time or another with their smartphones, about a third of all members also access Facebook from their desktop or notebook computers. That's where we start our journey— looking at how to use Facebook's website on your computer.

Understanding Social Networking

Facebook is a *social network*. A social network is an Internet-based service that hosts a community of users and makes it easy for those users to communicate with one another. Social networks enable users to share experiences and opinions with one another and thus keep in touch with friends and family members, no matter where they're located.

The goal of a social network is to create a network of online "friends" and then share your activities with them via a series of message posts. These posts are short messages, called *status updates*, which can be viewed by all your friends on the site. A status update can be text only, or it can contain photos, videos, and links to other web pages.

Your online friends read your posts, as well as posts from other friends, in a continuously updated stream. On Facebook, this stream is called the *News Feed*, and it's the one place where you can read updates from all your online friends and family; it's where you find out what's really happening.

There are many social networks on the Internet, but Facebook is the largest. (Other popular social networks include Instagram, LinkedIn, Pinterest, and Twitter.) Facebook was launched by Mark Zuckerberg while he was a student at Harvard in 2004. Facebook (originally called "thefacebook") was originally intended as a site where college students could socialize online. Sensing opportunity beyond the college market, Facebook opened its site to high school students in 2005, and then to all users over age 13 in 2006.

Although Facebook started as a network for college students, today it's the social network of choice for users of all ages. In fact, 65 percent of all people in the U.S. aged 50 to 64 (and 41 percent of those over 65) make Facebook their hub for all online social activity.

Signing Up for Facebook from Your Computer

To use Facebook, you first need to create a personal Facebook account. A Facebook account is free and easy to create; there's no fee to join and no monthly membership fees.

Create a New Facebook Account

You can create a Facebook account from either the Facebook website or the Facebook mobile app on your phone or tablet. Typing in your information from a computer is a little easier than doing so on your phone, so this section covers the website signup.

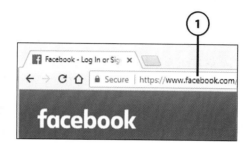

1. Use Google Chrome, Microsoft Edge, or another web browser to go to Facebook's home page at www.facebook.com.

2. Go to the Create a New Account section and enter your first name into the First Name box.

3. Enter your last name into the Last Name box.

4. Enter your email address or mobile phone number into the Mobile Number or Email box and, if asked to confirm, re-enter it into the next box. (Most people register with their email address, although you might want to use your mobile number if you only use Facebook on your smartphone.)

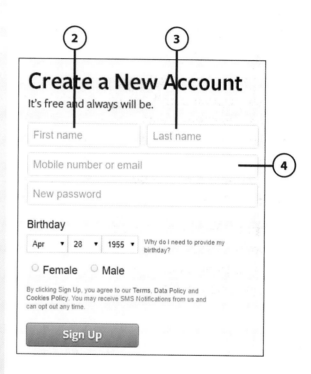

Email Address

Facebook uses your email address or phone number to confirm your identity and to contact you when necessary. You also use your email address or phone number to sign into Facebook each time you enter the site.

5 Enter your desired password into the New Password box. Your password should be at least six characters in length—the longer the better, for security reasons.

6 Select your date of birth from the Birthday list. (You can later choose to hide this information if you want; see Chapter 18, "Managing Your Facebook Account—Even When You're Gone," to learn how.)

7 Check the appropriate option for your gender.

8 Click the Sign Up button.

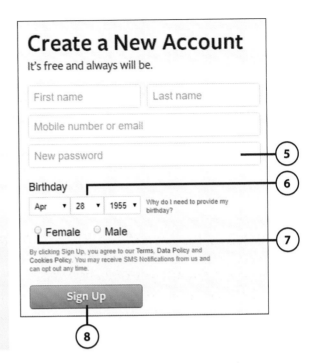

>>>**Go Further**

PASSWORD SECURITY

To make your password harder for hackers to guess, include a mix of alphabetic (upper- and lowercase), numeric, and special characters, such as punctuation marks. You can also make your password more secure by making it longer; an eight-character password is much harder to crack than a six-character one. Just remember, though, that the more complex you make your password, the more difficult it might be for you to remember—which means you probably need to write it down somewhere, just in case. (Just make sure wherever you write it down is kept well hidden and secure!)

>>>Go Further

EMAIL CONFIRMATION AND MORE

After you click the Sign Up button, Facebook sends you an email or text message asking you to confirm your new Facebook account. When you receive this message, click the link to proceed.

You're prompted to find friends who are already on Facebook and to fill in a few personal details for your profile page. You can perform these tasks now or later (which is probably more convenient), as I discuss later in this book.

Signing In—and Out—of the Facebook Website

After you've created your Facebook account, you can sign into the website and start finding new (and old) friends. You sign in at the same page you created your account—www.facebook.com.

Log On to the Facebook Site

You use your email address or phone number—and the password you created during the signup process—to log in to your Facebook account. When you're logged in, Facebook displays your home page.

(1) Use Google Chrome, Microsoft Edge, or another web browser to go to Facebook's home page at www.facebook.com.

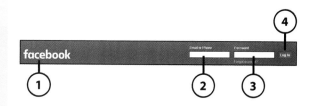

(2) Enter your email address or phone number into the Email or Phone box at the top of the page.

(3) Enter your password into the Password box.

(4) Click the Log In button. Or...

5 If you've previously logged in, you may see your picture in a tile on the Facebook login page. Click this tile to log on directly to your account.

Log Out of Your Facebook Account

You probably want to log out of Facebook if you're not going to be active for an extended period of time. You also want to log out if someone else in your household wants to access his or her Facebook account.

1 From any Facebook page, click the down arrow button on the far right of the toolbar.

2 Click Log Out from the drop-down menu.

Sign Back In

After you've logged out, you need to sign back in before you can access your Facebook content again.

Finding Your Way Around the Facebook Website

You discover more about using Facebook throughout the balance of this book, but for now let's examine how to get around the Facebook website. When it comes to moving from place to place on Facebook's site, you have two choices. You can use either the Facebook toolbar that appears at the top of every page, or the navigation pane that's displayed on the left side of all pages. Not all options are found in both places.

Navigate Facebook's Home Page

After you sign into your Facebook account on your computer, you see Facebook's home page. This page looks a little different for each user, as it displays content personalized for you.

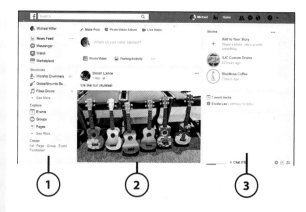

1. On the left side of the page is the *navigation sidebar*, or what Facebook imaginatively calls the *left side menu*. You use the options here to go to various places on the Facebook site.

2. The large column in the middle of the home page displays your *News Feed*, a stream of posts from all your Facebook friends. (It also includes posts from companies, celebrities, and groups you've followed.) At the top of this column is a box you use to post your own status updates.

3. The column on the right side of the page displays various Facebook notices and advertisements.

Use the Facebook Toolbar

The toolbar that appears at the top of every Facebook page is your primary means of navigating the Facebook site. The toolbar also provides notification when you have messages waiting or if a friend engages you in a specific activity.

1 Search the Facebook site for people or things by entering your query into the Search box; click the search (magnifying glass) icon or press Enter on your computer keyboard to start the search.

2 Click your name to view your personal profile page.

3 If you have multiple Facebook users on this computer, click the Account Switcher button to switch to another user's account.

4 Click the Home button at any time to return to the Home page.

5 If your toolbar displays the Find Friends button (it probably does if you're new), click it to view suggested people for your Facebook friends list.

6 Click the Friend Requests button to view any friend requests you've received and to search for new friends on the Facebook site.

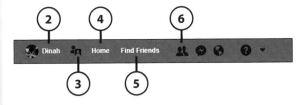

7 Click the Messages button to view your most recent private messages from Facebook friends.

8 Click the Notifications button to view notifications from Facebook, such as someone commenting on your status or accepting your friend request.

9 Click the Quick Help icon to get help using various Facebook options, as well as access important privacy settings. (Read more about privacy settings in Chapter 9, "Managing Your Privacy on Facebook.")

10 Click the down arrow button at the far right to access all sorts of account settings. This is also where you sign out of Facebook when you're done using it for the day.

Counting Requests and Messages

If you have pending friend requests, you see a white number in a red box on top of the Friend Requests button. (The number indicates how many requests you have.) Similarly, a white number in a red box on top of the Messages or Notifications buttons indicates how many unread messages or notifications you have.

Navigate with the Left Side Menu

You can get to even more features on Facebook when you use the navigation sidebar on the left side of the screen. Click any item to display that specific page.

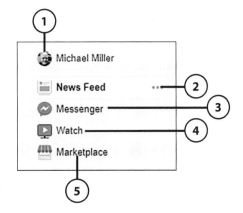

1. To visit your personal profile page, click your picture at the top of the menu. To edit your profile that appears on the profile page, click the More (three-dot) button and click Edit Profile.

2. To read posts from your Facebook friends, click News Feed. To switch your News Feed from the default Top Stories display to instead display your friends' most recent posts, click the More button next to News Feed and click Most Recent.

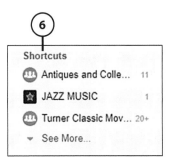

3. To view messages in your Facebook inbox or send a private message to another user, click Messenger.

4. To watch Facebook videos, click Watch.

5. To view items for sale in the Facebook Marketplace, click Marketplace.

6. Your favorite Facebook groups are listed in the Shortcuts section. Click the name of a group to view that group's page; click See More to expand this section to see more options.

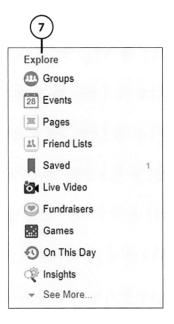

7. The Explore section includes links to all your Facebook events, groups, Pages, and more. Click an icon to view all items of that type; click See More to expand this section.

Use the Right Side Menu

The column on the right side of Facebook's Home page contains some items you might find useful and some you might not.

(1) The top of the column displays Facebook Stories—short photo and video collections from your friends that disappear after you've viewed them twice or 24 hours go by, whichever happens first. Click a Story to view it.

(2) Next are any events you've been invited to or friends who have upcoming birthdays.

(3) At the bottom-right corner of the Facebook window is the Chat bar. Click this to display a Chat list of friends who are currently online and free to chat. Click a name to initiate a chat session with that person.

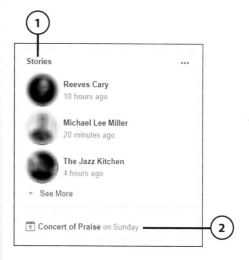

Widescreen Displays

If your computer display (and browser window) is wide enough, Facebook actually displays *four* columns. The fourth column displays the full Chat list, and the Chat bar does not then display at the bottom of the screen.

Facebook iPhone app

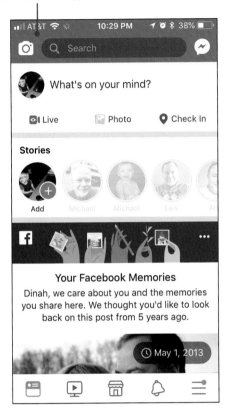

Facebook
iPad app

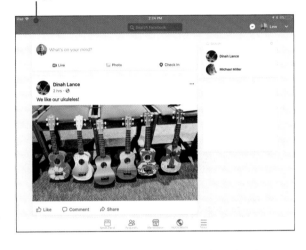

Facebook Android app

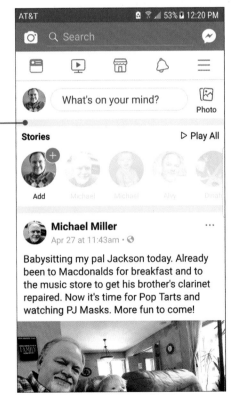

In this chapter, you find out how to use
Facebook on your smartphone or tablet.

→ Using Facebook's iPhone App
→ Using Facebook's iPad App
→ Using Facebook's Android App

2

Getting to Know Facebook on Your Mobile Device

Facebook reports that almost all (95 percent) of its users access its service, at least some of the time, via smartphones and tablets. Chances are that you'll do a lot of your Facebooking with a mobile device; it's the easy and convenient way to check in on your friends and family wherever you are.

When you use Facebook on your phone or tablet, you do so with Facebook's mobile app. Facebook has mobile apps for the iPhone, iPad, and Android devices. All these apps offer similar functionality, with slightly different layouts, so you don't have to wait until you get home to check your Facebook News Feed—or post a status update or photo!

Using Facebook's iPhone App

You can find Facebook's iPhone app in Apple's iPhone App Store. Just search the store for "Facebook" and download the app—it's free.

Logging In

The first time you launch any Facebook mobile app, you need to log into your account, if you already have one; tap either your name and picture or Log Into Another Account. If you don't yet have a Facebook account, enter your email address or mobile phone number, along with your password, and follow the onscreen instructions from there.

Navigate Facebook's iPhone App

When you first open Facebook's iPhone app you see the News Feed screen. This is a good starting place for all your Facebook-related activity.

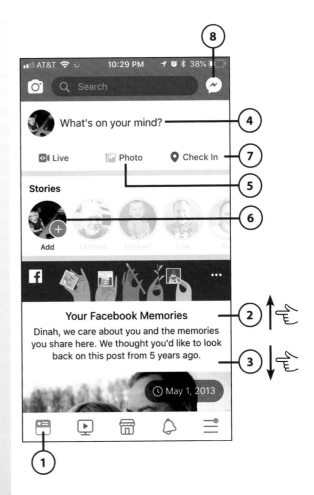

(1) Tap the News Feed icon at any time to display the News Feed screen.

(2) Swipe up to scroll down the screen and view older posts.

(3) Refresh the News Feed by pulling down the screen.

(4) Tap within the What's On Your Mind? box to post a status update.

(5) Post a photo by tapping Photo.

(6) View a story by tapping an icon in the Stories row.

(7) Tap Check In to "check in" (post your location only).

(8) Tap the Messenger icon to open the Messenger app and chat with online friends. (If you don't yet have the Messenger app installed on your phone, you'll be prompted to download it.)

It's Not All Good

Beware Stalkers

Using the Check In feature to broadcast your current location can alert any potential stalkers where to find you—or tell potential burglars that your house is currently empty. Because of the potential dangers, think twice about using this feature.

(9) To watch Facebook videos, tap the Watch icon.

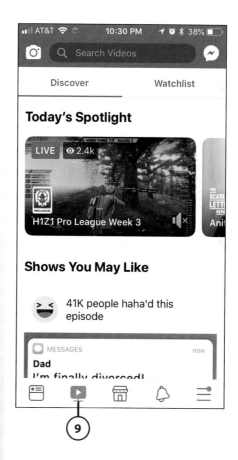

10 To view items for sale in the Facebook marketplace, tap the Marketplace icon.

11 To view notifications from Facebook, tap the Notifications icon.

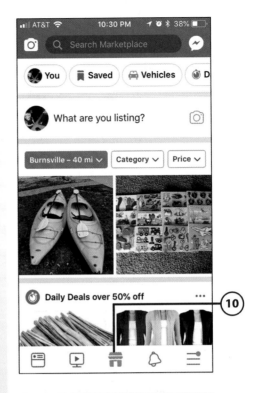

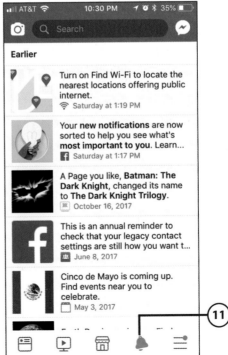

12 To view your favorite groups, pages, and more, tap the More icon.

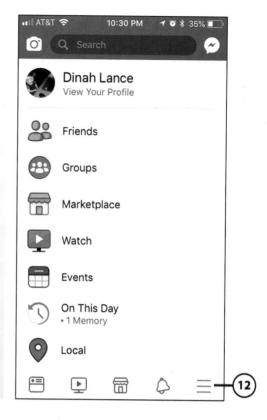

Using Facebook's iPad App

Facebook looks a little different on the bigger iPad screen than it does on the iPhone. It still does all the same things but with a slightly different layout.

Navigate Facebook's iPad App

When you first open the Facebook app on your iPad, you see the News Feed screen. This screen looks different depending on how you're holding your iPad.

(1) In landscape mode (held horizontally), you see the News Feed on the left with a sidebar on the right side of the screen that displays upcoming events, the Chat panel (with favorite friends listed), and more. Swipe up to scroll down the screen to view more updates in the News Feed.

(2) In portrait mode (held vertically), you see the normal screen with no additional sidebars. All the navigation icons are at the bottom of the screen; tap News Feed to display the News Feed.

(3) Refresh the News Feed by pulling down the screen.

(4) Tap What's On Your Mind? to post a status update.

(5) Tap Photo to post a photo.

(6) Tap Check In to "check in" (post your location only).

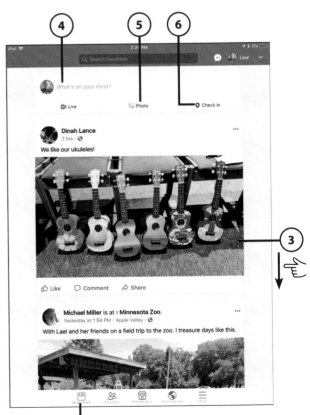

7. Tap the Messenger icon to open the Messenger app and chat with online friends. (If you don't yet have the Messenger app installed on your iPad, you'll be prompted to download it.)

8. Tap the down arrow in the top-right corner to access app settings.

9. Tap the Requests icon to view and respond to friend requests.

10 Tap the Marketplace icon to view items for sale in the Facebook Marketplace.

11 Tap the Notifications icon to view notifications from Facebook.

(12) Tap the More icon to view your pages, groups, events, and more.

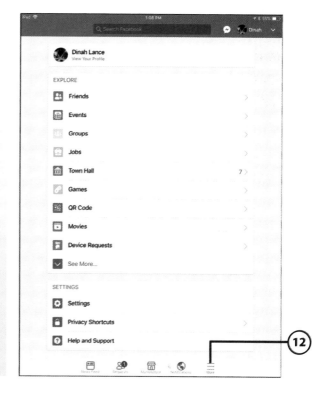

Using Facebook's Android App

If you use an Android phone or tablet, Facebook has a mobile app for you, too. You can find Facebook's Android app in the Google Play Store; just search the store for "Facebook" and download the app—it's free.

Navigate Facebook's Android App

The Facebook app for Android looks a lot like the Facebook app for iPhone, except the navigation icons are at the top of the screen instead of the bottom.

1. Tap the News Feed icon to display the News Feed.

2. Swipe up to scroll down the screen to view more updates from your friends.

3. Refresh the News Feed by pulling down from the top of the screen and then releasing.

4. Tap What's On Your Mind? to post a status update.

5. Tap Photo to post a photo.

6. Tap to view a story in the Stories row.

7. Tap the Watch icon to view Facebook videos.

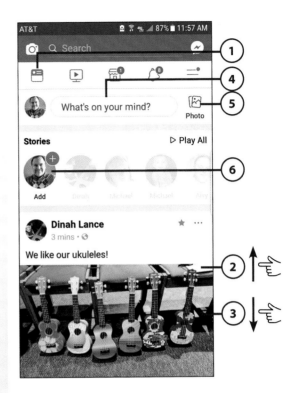

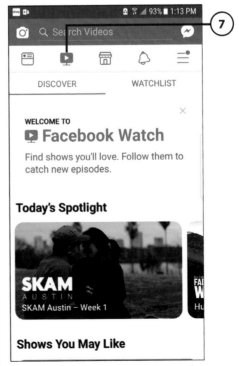

8 Tap the Marketplace icon to view items for sale in the Facebook Marketplace.

9 Tap the Notifications icon to view notifications from Facebook.

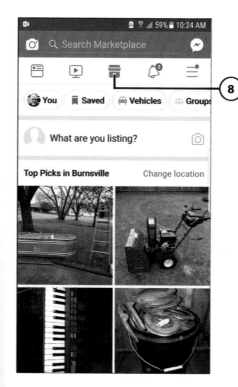

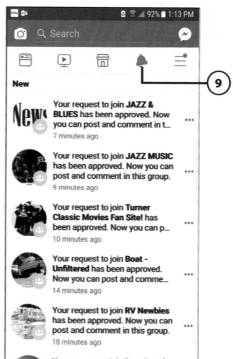

(10) Tap the More icon to view your pages, groups, and events, and to configure app settings.

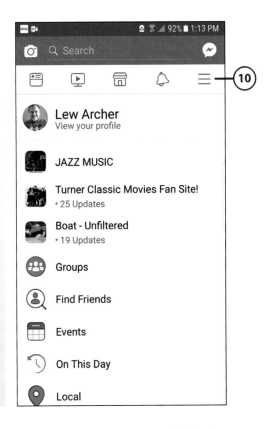

Mobile Website

You can also access Facebook using the web browser on your phone or tablet. Just enter the URL www.facebook.com and you'll see the mobile version of Facebook's website. When you access the mobile site from your phone, it looks a lot like the mobile app; access it from your iPad and it looks more like the normal Facebook website.

>>>Go Further

DESKTOP SITE OR MOBILE APP?

The content on Facebook is pretty much the same whether you use the mobile app on your phone or tablet, or you use the Facebook website on your desktop or notebook computer. So, what's the best way to access Facebook?

Obviously, if you want to access Facebook when you're on the go, the mobile app on your smartphone is the only way to go. Many users also use the mobile app when they're at home, just because it's more convenient to pull out your smartphone than it is to settle in behind a computer.

There are some things, however, that are easier to do on the larger computer screen using the computer keyboard. Writing long posts, for example, is easier to do on a computer keyboard. Some configuration settings are also easier to access from the Facebook website. And if you want to sort your News Feed by recent posts, you can do that only on the website.

Other than these operations, however, it's just as easy to use the mobile app as it is to access the website. And if you appreciate the convenience of having Facebook in the palm of your hand, the smartphone app is definitely the way to go.

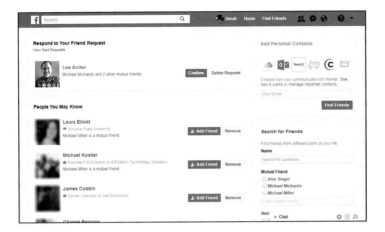

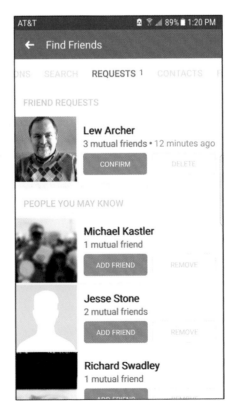

In this chapter, you find out how to locate people you know on Facebook and add them to your friends list.

→ Finding Facebook Friends
→ Accepting or Declining Friend Requests
→ Controlling What You See from Your Friends

3

Finding Friends on Facebook

Facebook is all about connecting with people you know. Anyone you connect with on Facebook is called a *friend*. A Facebook friend can be a real friend, or a family member, colleague, acquaintance... you name it. When you add people to your Facebook friends list, they can see everything you post—and you can see everything they post.

Of course, before you can make someone your Facebook friend, you have to find that person on Facebook. That isn't always as easy as you might think, especially when you're looking for people you went to school with or worked with several decades ago. People move, women might change their names when they get married (or divorced, or remarried, or some combination of the above), and it just becomes more difficult to find people over time. It might be difficult, but if they're on Facebook, you can probably find them.

Finding Facebook Friends

Because it's in Facebook's best interests for you to have as many connections as possible, the site makes it easy for you to find potential friends. This process is made easier by the fact that Facebook already knows a lot about you, based on the information you entered when you first signed up.

Facebook automatically suggests friends based on your personal history (where you've lived, worked, or gone to school), mutual friends (friends of people you're already friends with), and Facebook users who are in your email contacts lists. You can then invite any of these people to be your friend; if they accept, they're added to your Facebook friends list.

Facebook Friends

As far as Facebook is concerned, everyone you know is a "friend"—even family members. So when we talk about Facebook friends, these could be your brothers and sisters, children or grandchildren, neighbors, people you work with, casual acquaintances, or even real friends.

Find Friends in the Facebook Mobile App

It's easy to find friends when you're using Facebook on your mobile phone or tablet. Just let Facebook make some suggestions—and then decide whether you want to accept them or not. (This example shows how it looks on Facebook's Android app; it works similarly on the iOS version, too.)

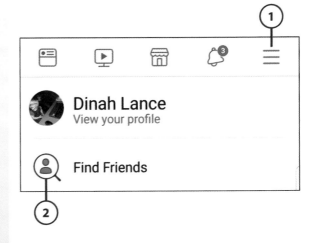

1 Tap the More icon to display the More screen.

2 Tap Find Friends.

3 Tap Requests. All pending friend requests are displayed at the top of the screen.

4 Tap Confirm to accept a request.

5 Scroll down the screen; suggested friends are displayed beneath the friend requests. Tap Add Friend to send that person a friend request.

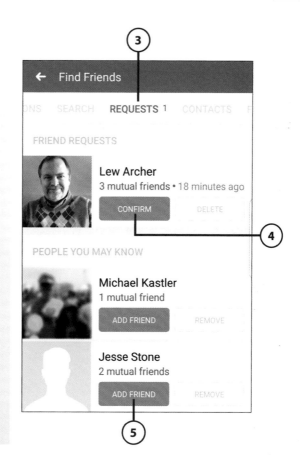

>>>Go Further

INVITATIONS

When you click the Add Friend button, Facebook doesn't automatically add that person to your friends list. Instead, that person receives an invitation to be your friend; she can accept or reject the invitation. If a person accepts your request, you become friends with that person. If a person does not accept your request, you don't become friends. (You are not notified if your friend request is declined.) In other words, you both have to agree to be friends—it's not a one-sided thing.

(6) To search for a specific friend, tap Search.

(7) Enter the name of the person you're looking for.

(8) Members who match your search are now displayed. Tap Add Friend to send a friend request.

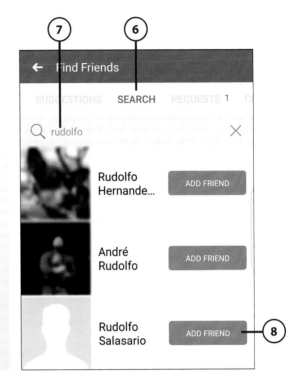

>>>Go Further

CONTACTS

Facebook can also look for members who are in your phone's contacts list. From the Find Friends screen, tap Contacts and then follow the onscreen instructions to allow Facebook access to your phone's contacts. All people in your contacts list who are also on Facebook are now listed. Tap Add Friend to send a friend request.

Find Friends on the Facebook Website

The friend-finding process is similar on Facebook's website—although you have a few more options when searching for friends.

How Many Friends?

Some people like to assemble a large list of Facebook friends, to keep in touch with everyone they've known throughout their lives. Other people find a large friends list somewhat overwhelming and prefer to keep a shorter list of close friends and family.

(1) On the Facebook website, click the Friend Requests button to display the drop-down menu.

(2) Any pending friend requests are listed first. Click the Confirm button to accept a request, or the Delete Request button to not accept it.

(3) Facebook also displays a list of suggested friends. Click the Add Friend button to send a friend request to a particular person.

(4) To search for more friends, click See All at the bottom of the menu. This displays a page that lists friend suggestions and various search options. (You can also get to this page by clicking the Find Friends button on the toolbar, if you have one; it's only displayed for newer users.)

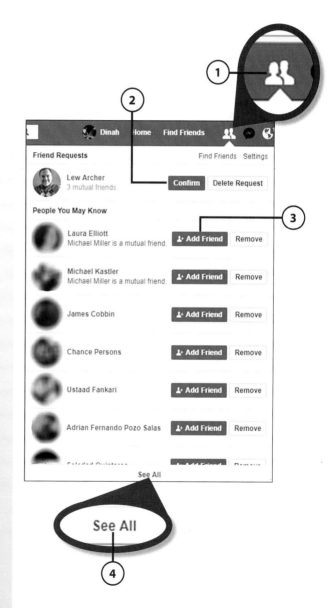

Suggested Friends

The people Facebook suggests as friends are typically people who went to the same schools you did, worked at the same companies you did, or are friends of your current friends.

5 In the right column of the page, scroll down until you see the Search for Friends panel. To search for someone by name, enter that person's name into the Name box.

6 To search for people who are already friends with your other Facebook friends, go to the Mutual Friend section and check the names of one or more friends. (If a particular friend isn't listed, enter his or her name into the text box first.)

7 To look for people who come from your hometown, go to the Hometown section and check your town. (If your hometown isn't listed, enter it into the text box first.)

8 To search for people who live near you now, go to the Current City section and check your city. (If your town or city isn't listed, enter it into the text box first.)

9 To search for people who went to the same high school you did, go to the High School section and check the name of your high school. (If your high school isn't listed, enter it into the text box first.)

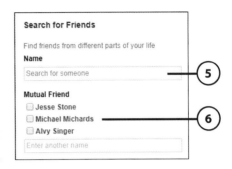

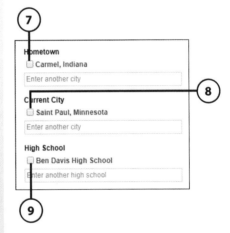

10 To search for people who went to the same college or university you did, go to the College or University section and check the name of your school. (If your school isn't listed, enter its name into the text box first.)

11 To search for people who work or worked at one of your current or former employers, go to the Employer section and check the name of that company. (If a company isn't listed, enter its name into the text box first.)

12 To search for former classmates who went to the same graduate school you did (if, in fact, you went to graduate school), go to the Graduate School section and check the name of that school. (If your grad school isn't listed, enter its name into the text box first.)

13 Whichever options you select, Facebook returns a list of suggested friends based on your selection. Click the Add Friend button to send a friend request to a specific person.

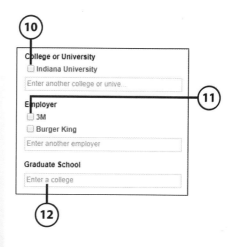

>>>Go Further
FIND EMAIL CONTACTS

Another way to find Facebook friends is to let Facebook look through your email contact lists for people who are also Facebook members. You can then invite those people to be your friends.

Facebook can search contacts from a variety of web-based email and communications services, including AOL Mail, Gmail, iCloud, and Yahoo! Mail.

To do this, click the Friends Request button to display the drop-down menu, and then click See All. On the top right of the Friends page you see the Add Personal Contacts panel. Click the logo for the email service or contacts application you use, or just enter your email address and click the Find Friends button. When prompted, enter your password and then follow the onscreen instructions.

This process works by matching the email addresses in your contact lists with the email addresses users provide as their Facebook login. When Facebook finds a match, it suggests that person as a potential friend.

Look for Friends of Friends

Another way to find old friends is to look for people who are friends of your current friends. That is, when you make someone your friend on Facebook, you can browse through the list of people who are on his friends list. Chances are you'll find mutual friends on this list—people that you both know but you haven't found otherwise.

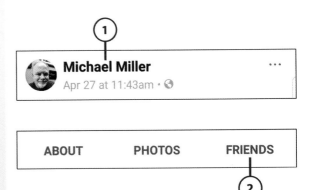

(1) Click or tap your friend's name anywhere on the Facebook site, such as in a status update, to display his profile page.

(2) Click or tap Friends under the person's name to display his Friends page, which lists all this person's Facebook friends.

(3) When you find a person you'd like to be friends with, click or tap the Add button.

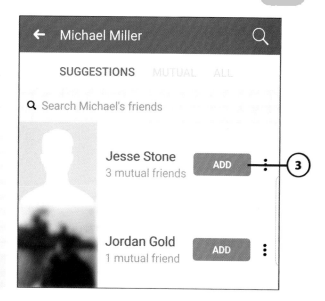

>>>Go Further

FINDING HARD-TO-FIND FRIENDS

When it comes to tracking down old friends on Facebook, sometimes a little detective work is in order. It's especially tough to find women you used to know, as names sometimes are changed along with marital status. Some women have enough forethought to enter their maiden name as their middle name on Facebook, so the Cathy Coolidge you used to know might be listed as Cathy Coolidge Smith, which means her maiden name actually shows up in a Facebook search. Others, however, don't do this—and thus become harder to find.

You can, of course, search for a partial name—searching just for "Cathy," for example. What happens next is a little interesting. Facebook returns a list of people named Cathy, of course, but puts at the top of this list people who have mutual friends in common with you. That's a nice touch, as it's likely that your old friend has already made a connection with another one of your Facebook friends.

Past that point, you can then display everyone on Facebook with that single name. But that's going to be a bit unwieldy, unless your friend has a unique name.

One approach to narrowing down the results is to filter your search results by location. For example, if you're looking for a John Smith and think he currently lives in Minnesota, use the Search Tools section to display only people named John Smith who live in Minnesota. You can also filter by school (Education) and employer (Workplace).

Beyond these tips, finding long-lost friends on Facebook is a trial-and-error process. The best advice is to keep plugging—if they're on Facebook, you'll likely find them sooner or later.

Accepting or Declining Friend Requests

Sometimes potential Facebook friends find you before you find them. When this happens, they will send you a friend request, which you can then accept or decline. You might receive a friend request via email, or you can view friend requests within Facebook.

Accept or Decline a Friend Request in the Facebook Mobile App

You don't need to access the Facebook website to see your pending friend requests. You can accept or decline friend requests directly from your mobile phone or tablet.

1. From within the mobile app, tap the More icon.

2. Tap Find Friends to display the Find Friends page.

3. Tap to display the Requests tab. All pending friend requests are listed here.

4. Tap Confirm to accept a given friend request.

5. Tap Delete to ignore the friend request.

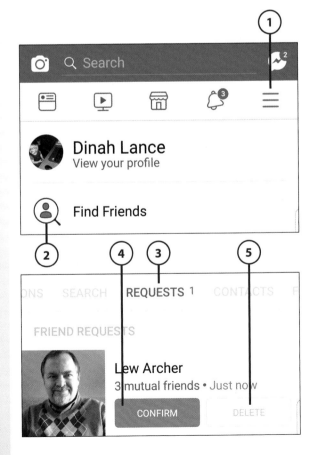

No One Knows

When you decline a friend request, the sender is not notified by Facebook. That person doesn't know that you've declined the request, just that you haven't (yet) accepted it.

Accept or Decline a Friend Request on the Facebook Website

You can also access all your pending friend requests from the Facebook website.

(1) Click the Friend Request button on the Facebook toolbar. All pending friend requests are displayed in the drop-down menu.

(2) Click Confirm to accept a specific friend request and be added to that person's friends list.

(3) Click Delete Request to decline a given request.

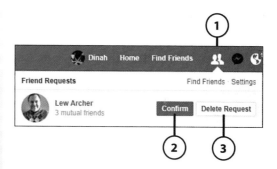

Controlling What You See from Your Friends

Not all Facebook friends are created equal. Some are closer than others; some aren't very close at all. Fortunately, you can control (to some degree) which friends you see more of in your News Feed. You can even unfollow or unfriend those friends you're no longer interested in!

Control Your News Feed

Facebook controls, to some degree, which posts show up in your News Feed. The more you interact with a given person, in terms of liking or commenting on her posts, the more posts from that person you'll see. If you don't respond much or at all to posts from a given friend, Facebook won't prioritize posts from that person in your News Feed.

This automatic customization of your News Feed aside, you can instruct Facebook to prioritize posts from certain friends—or even stop displaying a person's posts entirely.

(1) Click or tap your friend's name anywhere on the Facebook site, such as in a status update, to display her profile page.

(2) In the mobile app, tap Friends. (On the website, click Following.)

(3) To make sure you always see this friend's posts, click or tap See First, if available. (Options differ between iOS, Android, and web versions.)

(4) To remove this person's posts from your News Feed but still maintain her as a friend, click or tap Unfollow.

Unfriend a Friend

What do you do about those friends you really don't want to be friends with anymore? Sometimes people drift apart, or you don't like that person's political views or inane posts. Whatever the reason, you don't want to read any more of that person's posts, and you want to delete him from your friends list.

Fortunately, you can at any time remove an individual from your Facebook friends list. This is called *unfriending* the person, and it happens all the time.

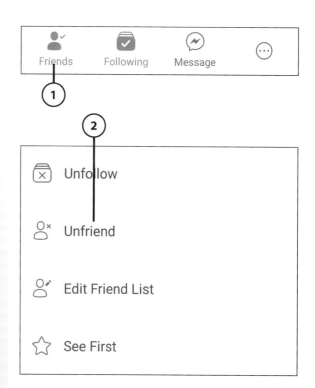

No One's the Wiser
When you unfriend people on Facebook, they don't know that they've been unfriended. There are no official notices sent.

(1) In the mobile app, go to the person's profile page and tap Friends.

(2) Tap Unfriend. (On the Facebook website, go to the person's profile page, click Friends, and then click Unfriend.)

Refriending
If you've unfriended someone but later want to add her back to your friends list, simply go through the add-a-friend process again.

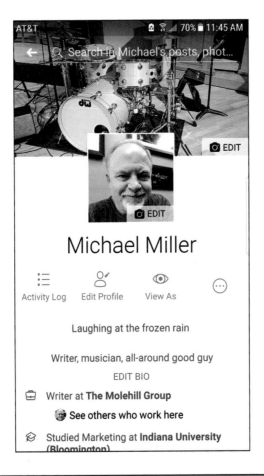

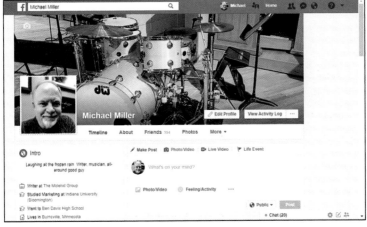

In this chapter, you find out how to personalize your Facebook profile page.

→ Viewing Your Profile
→ Changing the Look and Feel of Your Profile
→ Editing the Contents of Your Profile

Personalizing Your Profile

When friends or family want to see what you've been up to, they turn to a single Facebook page—your personal profile. Your profile page hosts all your personal information and status updates so that friends and family can learn all about you at a glance. Fortunately, you have some control over what gets displayed on your profile—it's your personal page on the Facebook site.

Viewing Your Profile

All your personal information, including the status updates you've posted, are displayed on your Facebook profile page. Your profile page is essentially your personal headquarters on Facebook, the place where all your Facebook friends can view your information and activity.

Timeline

A Facebook profile page is sometimes called a Timeline because it includes all the posts you've made over time.

Access Your Profile in the Facebook Mobile App

Your profile page looks a little different in the Facebook mobile app than it does on the Facebook website. It's nothing major; the information is simply configured for the smaller size of a mobile phone screen. (This example shows how it looks on the Android app.)

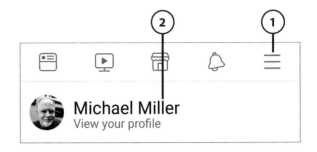

1. Tap the More button.

2. Tap your name to open your profile page.

3. Swipe up to scroll down the page and view all your information and status updates.

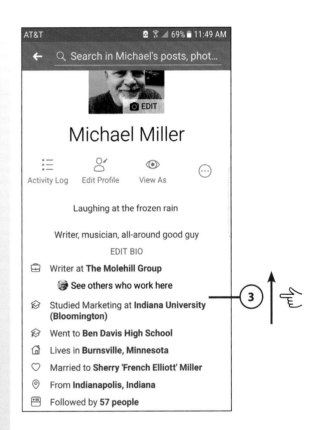

Access Your Profile on the Facebook Website

Your profile page on the Facebook website is designed in a two-column format, with basic information on the left and status updates on the right.

1. Click your name in either the Facebook toolbar or the navigation sidebar.

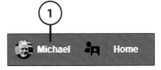

2 Scroll down the page to view all your information and status updates.

3 Click a tab to view that specific information.

Changing the Look and Feel of Your Profile

Facebook lets you personalize your profile page in a few different ways. You can add a profile picture of yourself, as well as a cover image that adorns the top of the page.

Change Your Profile Picture from the Facebook Mobile App

Your profile page includes your account's profile picture—and this is the first thing many people change. Your profile picture is an image of your choosing (it can be a picture of you or of anything, really) that appears not only on your profile page but also accompanies every post you make on the Facebook site. (For example, your profile picture appears in your friends' News Feeds, alongside each of your status updates.)

You can easily change the image that appears as your profile picture. Some users change this image frequently; others find a photo they like and stick to it.

(1) Open your profile page and tap your profile picture. (If you don't yet have a picture, tap the generic icon that's there, instead.)

(2) Select a photo from your phone by tapping Select Profile Picture to display pictures on your phone.

(3) Select an existing photo by navigating to and tapping the photo you want to use. Or…

(4) Take a new photo with your phone's camera by tapping the Camera Roll tab and then tapping the Camera tile or icon (this could be a "live" photo in the upper-left corner) and then taking a picture.

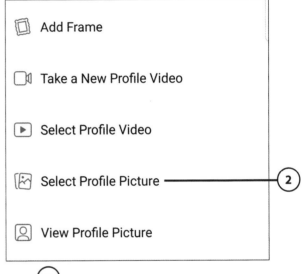

Add Frame

Take a New Profile Video

Select Profile Video

Select Profile Picture

View Profile Picture

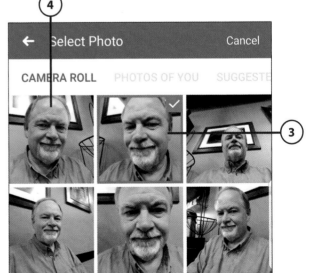

5 Tap Edit to make changes to this picture. You can crop the picture to better feature your face or add stickers, text, and doodles.

6 Tap Make Temporary to make this a temporary profile photo. *Or…*

7 Tap Use to use this photo. Your profile picture is now changed.

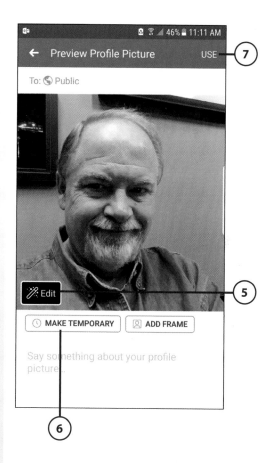

Add a Frame

You can also add a creative frame to your profile photo. On Facebook, a frame is more than just a literal frame; frames often add visual effects, text, and more to your profile photo.

1 In the Facebook mobile app, open your profile page and tap your profile picture.

2 Tap Add Frame.

3 Tap the kind of frame you want to add.

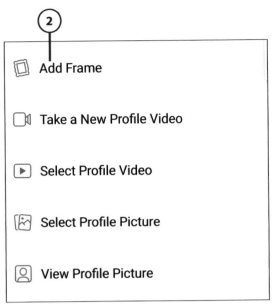

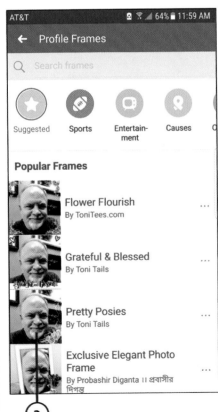

4 Tap Edit to crop your picture within the frame.

5 Tap Make Temporary to add the frame temporarily.

6 Tap Use to add the frame to your profile photo.

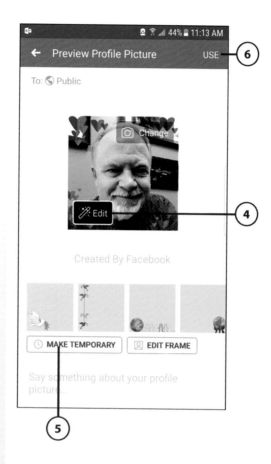

Change Your Profile Picture from the Facebook Website

You can just as easily choose a picture stored on your computer to use as your profile picture.

1 Open your profile page, mouse over your profile picture, and click Update Profile Picture to display the Update Profile Picture panel. (If you don't yet have a picture, click the generic icon that's there, instead.)

2 Click one of the suggested photos, if it's one you want to use. *Or…*

3 Choose another photo on your computer by clicking Upload Photo and then selecting the photo you want to use.

4 Use the slider to zoom into or out of the photo.

5 Drag the photo to reposition the contents.

6 Make this profile picture temporary by clicking the Make Temporary button, selecting when to switch back to your previous photo, and then clicking Save.

7 To make this your permanent profile picture (although you can change it anytime in the future), click Save.

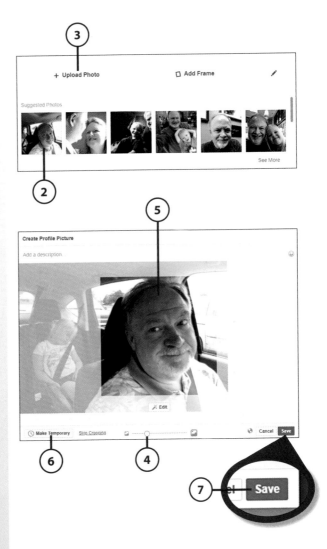

Add a Profile Video

If you're using the Facebook mobile app, you can make a video your profile picture. You can take or upload videos up to seven seconds in length; the video will display on a continuous loop on your profile page.

1 From within the mobile app, open your profile page and tap your profile picture.

2 Tap Take a New Profile Video. (To select from an existing video on your phone, tap Select Profile Video.)

3 By default, Facebook prepares to take a selfie video. To take a video with your phone's rear-facing camera, tap the Switch icon.

4 Tap the red Record button to start recording.

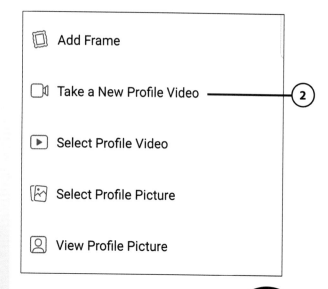

Add Frame

Take a New Profile Video — **2**

Select Profile Video

Select Profile Picture

View Profile Picture

5 Your camera automatically shoots a seven-second video and then stops recording. Tap Edit to trim, crop, or select a thumbnail from this video.

6 Tap Make Temporary to make this video temporary on your profile page.

7 Tap Use to make this video your profile picture.

Add a Cover Image from the Facebook Mobile App

By default, your profile picture appears against a shaded background at the top of your profile page—not very visually interesting. You can, however, select a background image (called a *cover image*) to appear on the top of the page. Many people choose landscapes or other artistic images that provide an interesting but non-obtrusive background to their profile picture; others choose more personal photos as their covers.

Cover Image Specs

Your cover image should be wider than it is tall. The ideal size is 851 pixels wide by 315 pixels tall—although if you upload a smaller or larger image, Facebook resizes it to fill the space.

---

1 Tap the existing cover image or, if you haven't yet added an image, the Add Cover Photo button.

(**2**) Tap Upload Photo. (Or, if you want to select from a photo you've previously uploaded, tap Select Photo on Facebook.)

(**3**) Navigate to and tap the photo you want to use.

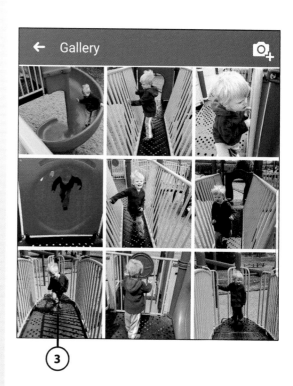

🖼 View Profile Cover

⬆ Upload Photo ————————— (2)

f Select Photo on Facebook

🖌 Select Artwork

◎ Take a 360 Cover Photo

← Gallery

(**3**)

(4) The photo is now previewed on your Timeline page. Drag the photo to reposition it, if necessary.

(5) Tap Save.

Use Facebook Artwork

In the Facebook Android app you can also select from artwork supplied by Facebook for your cover photo. After you tap the existing cover photo, tap Select Artwork and then make your choice.

Take a 360-Degree Cover Photo

You can also use your phone to take a 360-degree panoramic photo for your cover photo.

(1) From within the mobile app, tap the existing cover image or, if you haven't yet added an image, the Add Cover Photo button.

(2) Tap Take a 360 Cover Photo.

(3) Line up your view with the onscreen grid.

(4) Tap the blue button.

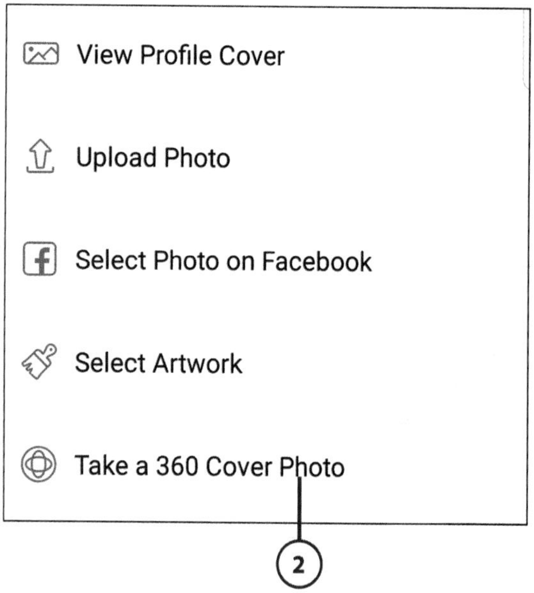

    View Profile Cover

    Upload Photo

    Select Photo on Facebook

    Select Artwork

    Take a 360 Cover Photo

(2)

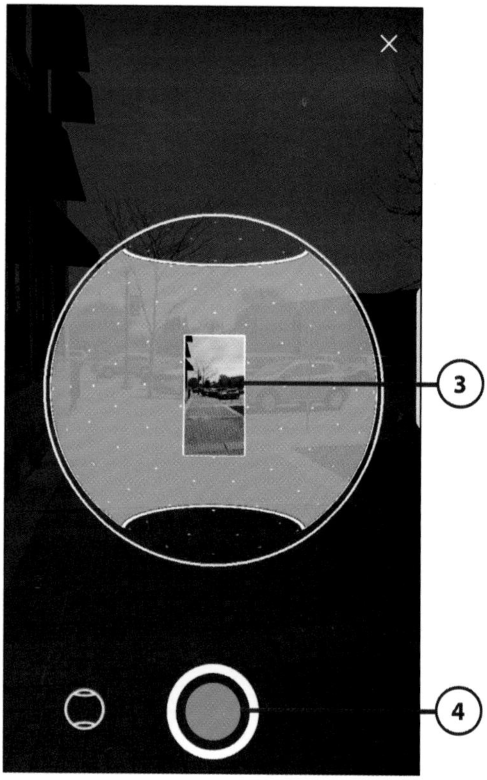

(3)

(4)

5. Move the camera left and/or right until you've shot an entire 360-degree view.

6. Tap the blue button when you're done.

7. Preview the cover image. Use your finger to move the image left and right.

8. Tap Save to save this panoramic photo as your cover photo.

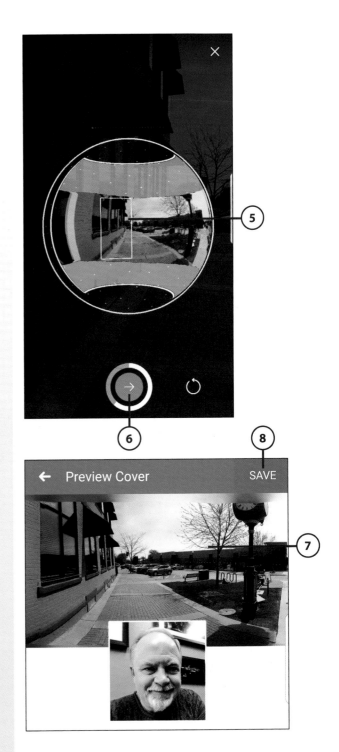

Add a Cover Image on the Facebook Website

It's just as easy to use a photo from your computer as the cover image, using the Facebook website.

(1) Open your profile page and mouse over the top-left corner of the existing cover photo or generic image, and then click the Add or Update Cover Photo button. A pop-up menu with several options displays.

(2) To select from a photo already uploaded to Facebook, click Select Photo.

(3) To select from supplied Facebook artwork, click Select Artwork.

(4) To upload a new photo from your computer, click Upload Photo.

(5) You're prompted to reposition the cover image by dragging it around the cover image space. Use your mouse to reposition the image as necessary.

(6) Click the Save Changes button.

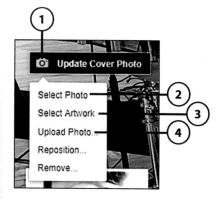

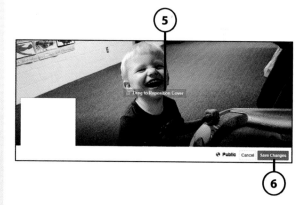

Reposition Your Cover Image

You can reposition the picture used as your cover image at any time. Mouse over your cover image, click Update Cover Photo, and then click Reposition. Use your mouse to position the image as you wish, and then click the Save Changes button.

Editing the Contents of Your Profile

You can edit most of the personal information displayed on your profile page, to either add new events or hide information you'd rather not leave public. You can also choose to hide unwanted status updates.

Update Your Profile Information

Many people don't fully complete their profiles when first joining Facebook. Maybe you forgot to include certain information, or maybe you entered it wrong. In any case, Facebook lets you easily edit or update the personal information in your Facebook profile. You can also select who can view what information.

The process of changing your profile info is similar whether you're using the Facebook mobile app or website.

>>>*Go Further*

THE MORE FACEBOOK KNOWS...

All the personal information that Facebook requests of you is optional—you don't have to enter it if you don't want to. For privacy reasons, you might share less. (Learn more in Chapter 9, "Managing Your Privacy on Facebook.") On the other hand, the more Facebook knows about you, the better it can suggest activities, groups, and friends. For example, Facebook makes more and more relevant friend suggestions when you add every school you've attended and every employer you've worked for. Of course, the more information you share with Facebook, the more Facebook can use that information for its own purposes. So share only that information you feel makes your experience more enjoyable.

(1) Go to your profile page and click or tap Edit Profile or Update Profile. This displays a special page for entering and editing your information.

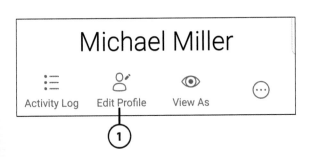

2 In the Facebook mobile app, scroll down to get to the section you want to edit, and then tap the Edit button for that section. For example, to edit the details in your Bio, tap Edit Details.

3 Tap the Edit (pencil) button for the item you want to edit.

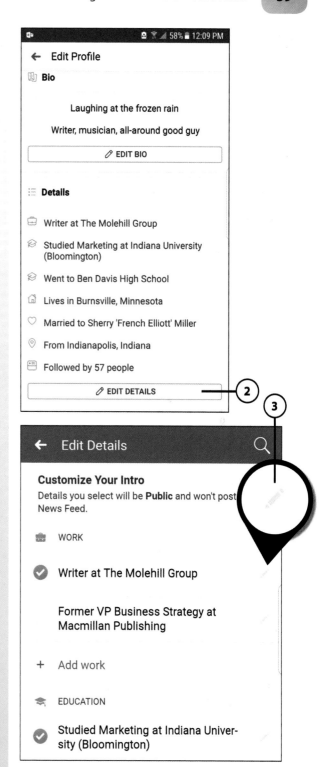

(4) Make your changes.

(5) Tap the Privacy button and then select who can view this information—Public, Friends, or More Options.

(6) Click Save when you're done editing.

(7) To add a new entry for a given section, click the + Add link for that item. For example, to add a new former workplace, tap + Add Work.

(8) Tap Save when done.

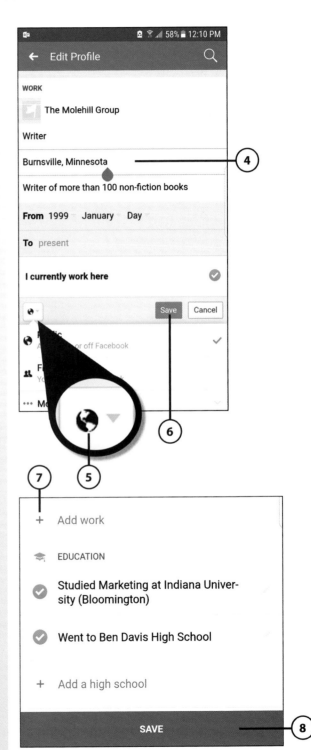

9 On the Facebook website, click the Edit (pencil) icon for the section you want to edit.

10 For the item you want to edit, mouse over the item, click Options, and then click Edit.

11 Make your changes.

12 Click the Privacy button, and then select who can view this information.

13 To add a new entry for a given section, click the + Add link for that item.

14 Click Save Changes when you're done editing.

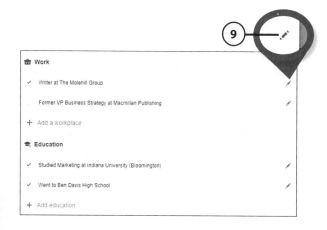

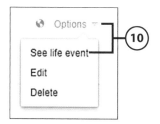

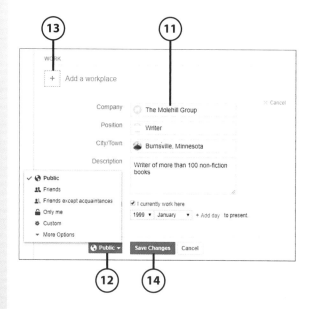

>>>Go Further
WHO KNOWS WHAT?

Not everyone viewing your profile needs to see all your information. For example, you might want everyone to view your birthdate, but not necessarily the year of your birth. You might want only your friends to view your relationship status, or you might not want to share your personal contact information with anyone. You can fine-tune your profile as granularly as you like, in this fashion, to create a clear division between your public and private lives.

Hide and Delete a Status Update

In addition to your personal information, your profile page displays all the status updates you've made on Facebook, from the first day you signed up to just now. You don't have to display every single status update, however; if there's an embarrassing update out there, you can choose to either hide it from view or completely delete it.

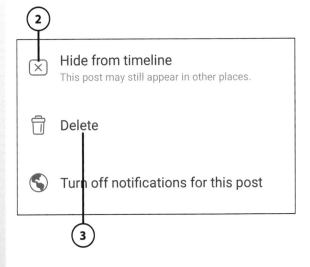

(1) Go to your profile page, scroll to a specific status update, and click or tap the More (three dot) icon in the top-right corner to display a menu of options.

(2) Click or tap Hide from Timeline to hide this update but not permanently delete it. (Hidden posts can be unhidden in the future.)

(3) Click Delete to permanently delete this update from Facebook. (Deleted posts cannot be undeleted.)

Not Everything Can Be Deleted

Not all status updates can be deleted. If the Delete option doesn't appear, you should opt to hide the update instead.

View and Edit All Your Facebook Activity

Your profile page presents all your Facebook activity in a nice, visually attractive fashion. However, if you want a more straightforward view of what you've done online, you can display and edit your Activity Log. This is a chronological list of everything you've done on the Facebook site, from status updates to links to comments you've made on others' posts.

>>>Go Further

CLEAN UP YOUR TIMELINE

Many users find the Activity Log the most efficient way to clean up entries on their Timelines. It's easier to see what's posted (and available to post) from the more condensed Activity Log listing than it is by scrolling through the individual posts on your profile page.

(1) From your profile page, click View Activity Log (on the website) or tap Activity Log (in the mobile app). This displays your Facebook Activity Log.

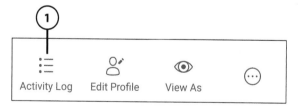

(2) In the mobile app, tap the down arrow for a post and then tap either Hide from Timeline, Show on Timeline (to unhide a previously hidden post), or Delete. (If the item is a "like" of another post, you have the option to Unlike that post.)

(3) To change who can view an item, tap Edit Privacy and make a new selection. (You can only change the privacy of your own posts.)

(4) On the Facebook website, click the Edit (pencil) button for an item.

(5) Check Hidden from Timeline to hide that item from your Timeline. To unhide a previously hidden item, check Allowed on Timeline. (If the item is a "like" of another post, you can select to Unlike that item.)

(6) To change who can view an item, click the Privacy button and make a new selection. (You can only change the privacy of your own posts.)

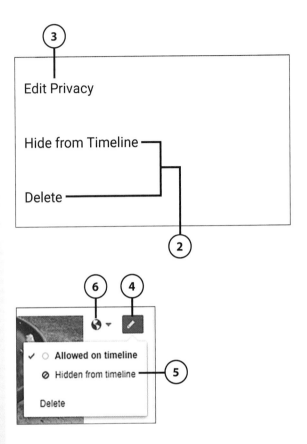

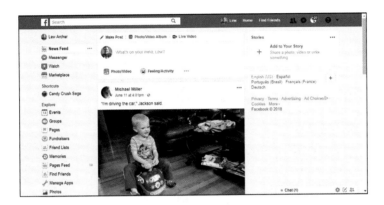

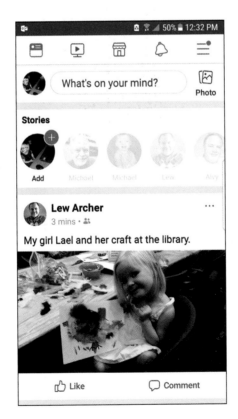

In this chapter, you discover how to read and respond to your friends' status updates in your Facebook News Feed.

→ Viewing Status Updates in the News Feed in the Facebook Mobile App
→ Viewing Status Updates on the Facebook Website
→ Personalizing Your News Feed
→ Exploring What Others Are Talking About
→ Viewing Your Friends' Stories
→ Viewing a Friend's Profile

Discovering What Your Friends and Family Are Up To

After you've added someone to your Facebook friends list, you'll be kept up to date on what that person is doing and thinking. Things that person posts to Facebook—text updates, photos, videos, you name it—automatically appear in your News Feed.

Viewing Status Updates in the Facebook Mobile App

Facebook's News Feed is where you keep abreast of what all your friends are up to. When a person posts a status update to Facebook, it appears in your personal News Feed. (The examples in this chapter use the Android app; the iPhone app works similarly.)

Display the Newsfeed

The News Feed is front and center in Facebook's mobile app; it's the default view when you open the app on your phone or tablet.

1. Tap the News Feed icon to display the News Feed.

2. Swipe up to scroll down the page and view more updates.

3. Pull down the screen to refresh the News Feed.

View a Status Update

The News Feed consists of status updates made by your friends and by company and celebrity pages you've liked on Facebook. It also includes posts from Facebook groups you've joined, as well as the occasional advertisement.

1. The poster's profile picture appears in the top-left corner of the status update.

2. The poster's name appears at the top of the post, beside the profile picture. To view the poster's profile page, tap the person's name.

3. When the item was posted (how many minutes or hours or days ago) is displayed beneath the poster's name.

④ The content of the status update appears under the top portion of the post. This can include text, images, or a video.

⑤ Links to like, comment on, and (depending on the content) share this post appear after the post content.

View a Link to a Web Page

Many status updates include links to interesting web pages. You can tap a link to view the web page posted by your friend.

① The title of the linked-to web page appears under the normal status update text. (Many links also include images from the linked-to page, as well as short descriptions of the pages' contents.) Tap the title or image to display the linked-to web page in a screen in the Facebook app.

(**2**) Tap the X (Android) or back arrow
(iOS) to return to the News Feed.

View a Photo

Many Facebook users post photos in
addition to or instead of text messages. You can view these photos in
the News Feed itself, or you can tap
the photos to view them larger on
your mobile device.

(**1**) Tap a picture to view it on its own
screen.

② Tap Like to like this photo.

③ Tap Comment to leave a comment on this photo.

④ Tap Share to share this photo with your Facebook friends. (This option might not be available; not every post can be shared.)

⑤ Tap the More (three dot) button and then tap Save Photo to download this photo to your phone or tablet.

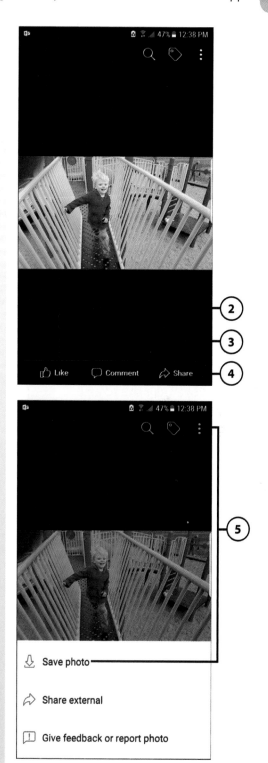

View a Video

Facebook users can also post videos to their News Feeds. These can be videos uploaded from their phones or videos uploaded to YouTube.

(1) Navigate to the status update that contains the video and then tap the video thumbnail to play the video.

(2) In some cases, video playback begins in the News Feed itself. In most instances, however, playback begins on a separate video page. Tap the Full-Screen icon to expand the video and view it full-screen.

(3) To pause playback, tap the screen to display the Pause button, and then tap the Pause button. Tap the Play button or tap the screen again to resume playback.

(4) To move to another point in the video, tap the screen to display the time slider, and then tap and drag the slider.

(5) Scroll down the page or tap the More Videos button to view similar videos. Tap your phone's Back button to return to your News Feed.

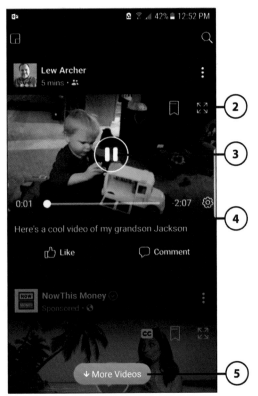

Videos from Other Sites

If someone has posted a video from YouTube, Vimeo, or another video-sharing site, playback probably takes place within the News Feed. To view the video on the YouTube or Vimeo site, click or tap the title of the video to open that site in a new tab in your device's web browser or in the appropriate app on your mobile device. (Tap the video itself, and it plays within the News Feed.)

Like an Update

Facebook offers several ways to "like" your favorite posts. You can give a post a simple "thumbs up" or apply other emojis to express your feelings.

Emojis

An emoji is a small digital image or icon used to express an emotion, idea, or opinion.

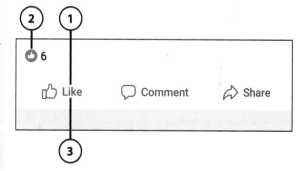

(1) To "like" a post, tap the Like icon; the thumbs-up icon turns blue. (If you tap Like by mistake, or later decide you really don't like it, tap the blue thumbs-up icon.)

(2) To view who else has liked this post, tap the Liked icon.

(3) To express a different emotion, tap and hold the Like icon to display a variety of emojis.

(4) Tap the emoji you want to apply.

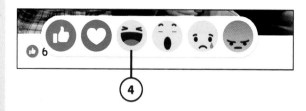

Comment on an Update

Want to share your opinions about a given status update? You can.

(1) View others' comments by tapping the Comments indicator.

(2) Leave your own comment by tapping the Comment icon to display the Write a Comment screen.

(3) Use your device's onscreen keyboard to enter your thoughts into the Write a Comment Box.

(4) Tap the Send icon to post your comments.

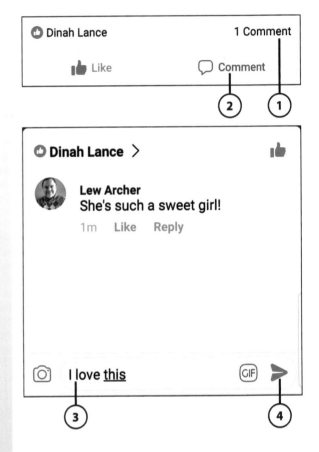

Share an Update

You can also share status updates in your News Feed with your other Facebook friends.

(1) Tap the Share icon. (If there's no Share icon present, you cannot share this particular post.)

(2) To share the post as-is, without any additional comments, tap Share Now (iOS) or Share Post Now (Android).

(3) To add your comments to the shared post, tap Write Post.

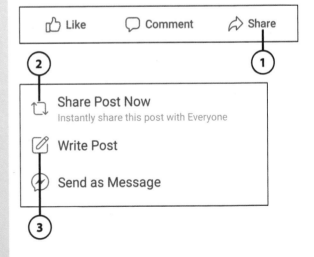

4 Use your device's onscreen keyboard to add your text comments.

5 Tap Post to repost the update to your friends.

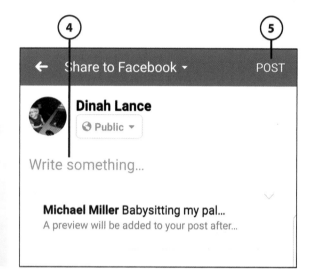

Viewing Status Updates on the Facebook Website

The News Feed and status updates work pretty much the same way on the Facebook website as they do in the mobile app. In fact, you have a few more options available when you access Facebook from your notebook or desktop computer.

Display the News Feed

You can easily get to the News Feed from anywhere on the Facebook site, using the ever-present toolbar at the top of every Facebook page.

1 From the Facebook toolbar, click the Home button. The News Feed displays in the center of the page.

2 The News Feed lists what Facebook deems to be your most relevant or interesting posts at the top. Scroll down to view additional posts.

View a Status Update

Each status update in your News Feed consists of several distinct components.

1. The poster's profile picture appears in the top-left corner.

2. The poster's name appears at the top of the post, beside the profile picture.

3. When the item was posted (how many minutes or hours or days ago) is displayed beneath the poster's name.

4. The content of the status update appears under the top portion of the post. This can include text, images, or a video.

5. Links to like, comment on, and share (available for certain content) this post appear after the post content.

6. To view more information about this person, mouse over his or her name; to view the poster's profile page, click the person's name.

View a Link to a Web Page

Many status updates include links to interesting web pages. You can click a link to view the web page posted by your friend.

(1) The title of the linked-to web page appears under the normal status update text. Click the title to display the linked-to web page in a new tab of your web browser.

(2) Many links include images from the linked-to page, as well as a short description of the page's content. (You can also click the image to go to the linked-to page.)

View a Photo

It's common for Facebook users to post photos of various types. These photos appear as part of the status update.

(1) The photo appears in the body of the status update. (If more than one photo is posted, they may appear in a tiled collage or in side-scrolling display.) To view a larger version of any picture, click the photo in the post.

2 This displays the photo within its own *lightbox*—a special window superimposed over the News Feed. Click the right arrow to view this user's next photo or click the left arrow to view the previous photo.

3 To close the photo lightbox, click the X in the upper-right corner.

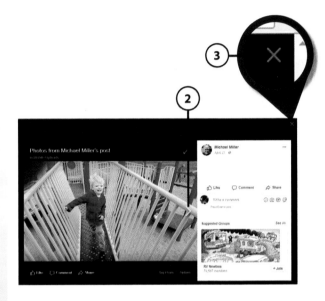

View a Video

Many Facebook users post videos shot with their smartphones so their friends can view them.

1 A thumbnail image from the video appears in the body of the status update. Some videos start playing automatically when the post is viewed. Others appear with a "play" arrow superimposed on top of the image; click the image to play the video.

2 If the video plays with the sound muted, mouse over the video to display the playback controls and then click the Volume (speaker) button and adjust the volume.

3 Pause playback by mousing over the video and then clicking the Pause button.

4 View the video full screen by clicking the full screen button.

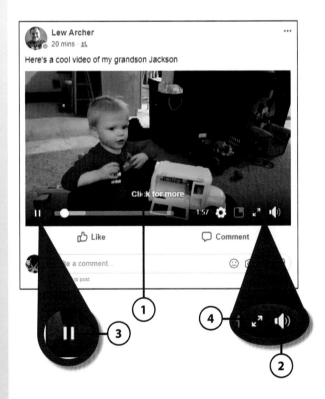

Like an Update

When you "like" a friend's status update, you give it a virtual "thumbs up." It's like voting on a post; when you view a status update, you see the number of "likes" that post has received.

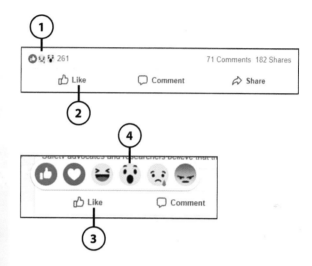

1. Click the Liked icon to view others who have liked this post.

2. To add a simple "like," click Like underneath the status update.

3. To express another emotion, mouse over the Like icon to view a selection of emojis.

4. Click the emoji you want to use.

Dislike and Unlike

While there is no corresponding "dislike" feature on Facebook, there is an Angry emoji that you can apply. You can also "unlike" any post you've previously liked; just click the colored Like icon to change your opinion.

Comment on an Update

Sometimes you want to comment on a given post, to share your thoughts about the post with your friend. You do this by leaving a public comment, which can then be seen by others viewing the original post.

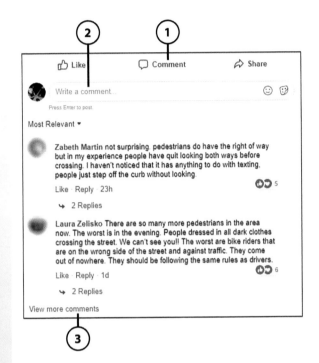

(1) Although you can click the Comment link below the post, in most cases that isn't necessary. (You only need to click Comment if the Write a Comment box is not visible beneath the post.)

(2) Type your comment into the Write a Comment box and press Enter.

(3) Comments made by other users appear underneath the original post. Click View More Comments to view additional comments.

Share an Update

Occasionally, you'll find a status update that is interesting or intriguing enough you want to share it with all your friends. You do this via Facebook's Share feature.

(1) Click Share underneath the original post to display a variety of sharing options. (Note that not all status updates can be shared.)

(2) Click Share Now to share without adding your own personal message.

(3) To add your comments to the shared post, click Share to display the Sharing panel.

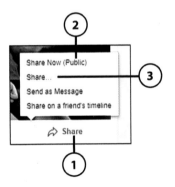

4 Enter any comments you might have on this post into the Say Something About This area.

5 Click the Post button.

>>>Go Further

SHARE PRIVATELY

If you'd rather share a post privately with selected friends, click Share and then select Send as Message. When the Share in a Private Message dialog box appears, enter the friends' names into the To section, write a short message, and then click the Send button.

Personalizing Your News Feed

By default, your News Feed displays what Facebook calls your Top Stories, selected by Facebook. To pick these Top Stories, Facebook uses some sort of ever-changing, super top-secret algorithm to determine which status updates are most important to you.

The operative word here is "tries." Facebook's various analyses and algorithms sometimes get it right but just as often feed you updates in which you have little interest, while at the same time hiding updates that might be important to you.

Fortunately, Facebook lets you manually fine-tune the items that appear in your News Feed, in a few different ways. If you find that your News Feed doesn't quite get it right, you might want to make these changes.

Display Most Recent Posts

Although the feature is somewhat hidden, you can change the News Feed to display your friends' most recent posts instead of those automatically selected Top Stories. The change won't stick from visit to visit, however, but you can always click the Most Recent option again.

1. On the Facebook website, click the More (three-dot) icon next to News Feed in the navigation sidebar, and then click Most Recent.

2. In the Facebook mobile app, tap the More button, and then tap Feeds.

3. Tap Most Recent.

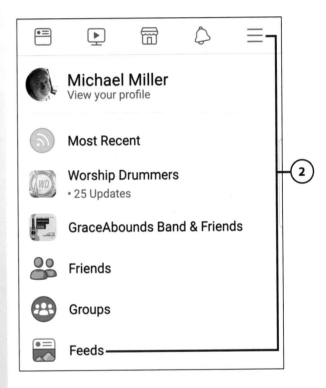

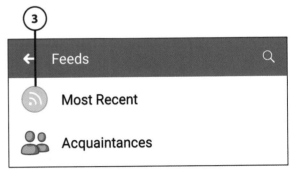

Hide Posts You Don't Like

Another way to train Facebook about what you like and don't like in your News Feed is to tell it to hide those posts that you don't really want to see. You can do this from any post you dislike.

1. Tap or click the More icon at the top-right corner of the post you don't like.

2. Tap or click Hide Post. This hides this particular post and tells Facebook to display fewer posts like this one.

>>>Go Further
SNOOZING AND HIDING FRIENDS

Sometimes you run into a Facebook friend who just gets to be a bit too much. I find this happens around election season, when I quickly tire of various friends' partisan rants. Fortunately, Facebook gives you several options for hiding posts from specific friends.

The first option is to "snooze" a friend's posts for a month. That is, all that person's posts are blocked from your News Feed for 30 days; the person remains on your friends list, but you don't have to listen to his or her rants for a while. After 30 days, that person's posts will automatically start showing up in your News Feed again.

To "snooze" a friend in this manner, just tap or click the More icon on one of this person's posts, and then click or tap Snooze *Friend* for 30 Days. That's all there is to it.

You also have the option of permanently removing all a friend's posts from your News Feed. You'll still be friends with this person; Facebook simply hides all that person's posts. To do this, tap or click the More icon on one of this person's posts and click or tap Unfollow *Friend*. (If you want to hide all posts from a person in a group you follow, tap or click Hide All from *Person*.)

Follow a Specific Post

Just as you can choose to hide posts you don't like, you can also choose to spotlight those posts in which you're particularly interested. Say you find a post that has a lively set of comments from other users, and you don't want to miss additional comments to that post. Facebook lets you receive notifications about that post—and have it pushed back up in your News Feed—when other users post their comments. In essence, you're telling Facebook that the status update—and all the comments on it—are important to you.

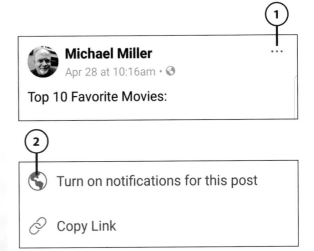

(1) Tap or click the More icon at the top-right corner of the post you want to follow.

(2) Tap or click Turn On Notifications for This Post. You now receive notifications when people add new comments to this post.

Configure News Feed Preferences

You can also personalize your News Feed by prioritizing whose posts you see first; unfollowing people whose posts you don't want to see; and reconnecting with people you previously unfollowed. The Facebook website even lets you discover Pages from companies and celebrities in which you might be interested.

(1) In the mobile app, tap the More icon and then scroll down and tap Settings & Privacy.

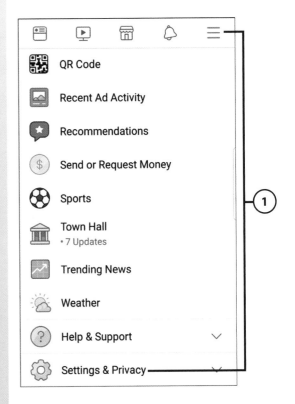

2 Tap Settings.

3 Scroll to the News Feed Settings section, tap News Feed Preferences, and then proceed to step 6. *Or…*

4 On the Facebook website, click the down arrow in the tool-bar and then click News Feed Preferences.

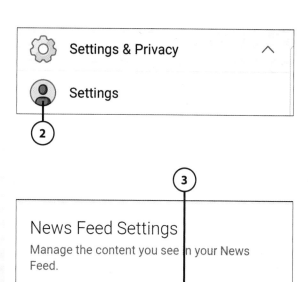

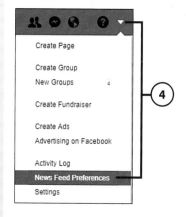

5 Put your favorite users at the top of the News Feed by clicking or tapping Prioritize Who to See First and then clicking or tapping those users.

6 Remove unwanted users from your News Feed by clicking or tapping Unfollow People to Hide Their Posts and then clicking or tapping those users you don't want to see.

7 Restore unfollowed users to your News Feed by clicking or tapping Reconnect with People You Unfollowed and then clicking or tapping the given user.

8 Add specific celebrity or company Pages to your News Feed by tapping Discover Pages That Match Your Interests.

9 Tap More Options (or click See More Options on the website) to show posts from apps otherwise hidden.

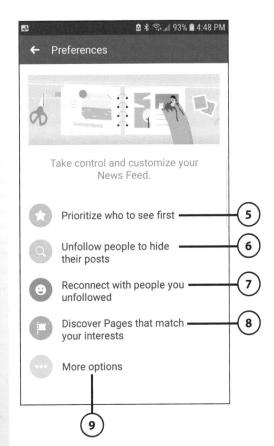

Exploring What Others Are Talking About

Everything goes in cycles—including Facebook posts. What was popular last year isn't so popular today.

The posts you're most likely to see in your News Feed reflect what other Facebook users like to see. Facebook uses a proprietary algorithm to determine what the "top stories" are in your Top Stories feed, but in general it's those types of posts that other users are most apt to like, share, or comment on.

What, then, is most likely to show up in your News Feed? It's all about things you can view at a glance, including the following:

- **Images:** Facebook started out as pretty much a text-only service, but that's changed; today, most posts are accompanied by some sort of visual, typically one or more photos. People prefer looking at pictures to reading text, so posts with pictures get viewed more often than those without. If you want your friends to see more of your posts, you need to post pictures in addition to your text. It certainly helps if the picture has something to do with what you're posting, and the more appealing the picture, the more eyeballs you'll attract. But the key thing is to get some sort of visual in as many posts as possible.

- **Memes:** A *meme* is a concept or catchphrase or image that spreads in a viral fashion across Facebook. While memes are essentially passing fads, they do get a lot of likes and shares, which boosts their popularity on Facebook. Chances are a meme you see in your News Feed today (and tomorrow and the next day) will wear out its welcome in a few weeks.

- **Surveys:** A specific type of meme that has become increasingly popular of late is the *survey*. This typically consists of a picture that boasts the results of someone taking the survey; you're prompted to click the picture or link to take the survey yourself. Most of these surveys are fun and not very scientific. There's little harm in taking one of these surveys, other than the time you waste doing so. The results are most often generic and seldom reflect any deep insights into your life or character.

It's Not All Good

Don't Share Too Much

I say that most surveys are harmless because they are. However, some companies use these types of surveys to collect data about you—which they then can use to target advertising at you or even share (for a profit) with other companies. (This was a source of controversy during the 2016 presidential election, where a company called Cambridge Analytica devised a Facebook survey that let it scrape personal information that was then used to target potential Donald Trump voters.)

Worst case, clever tricksters can shape surveys to get information they can then use to try to crack your password. (Such as what is your pet's name, or favorite TV show, or other such thing that might commonly be used as a password.) So, taking this type of survey could be fun, or it could be a way to trick you out of providing valuable personal information. As with everything online these days, be wary!

- **Countdown lists:** Another popular type of post is the quasi-informational list that purports to tell you X number of things about a given topic. These posts come with sensational headlines designed to grab you and pull you in, such as "18 Reasons We'll Always Be Crazy for Patrick Swayze" or "10 Bad Movie Ideas" or "12 Best Celebrity Beach Bodies." What these posts do is take you to another website, where each of the X number of things has its own page. You have to click from page to page to view all the items on the countdown list, and each page is chock full of ads. It's all a big scam to get you to click one of the ads (either on purpose or accidentally) so the host site can generate money from that advertising. There's no actual harm done—again, it's just a waste of your time.

- **Links to web pages:** Many of your Facebook friends post links to other interesting information on the Web. A post with a web page link is typically accompanied by a thumbnail image from that page, so the post is visual and gets your attention.

- **Games:** If your friends play a lot of games on Facebook, chances are you'll see a lot of posts from or about those games in your News Feed. These games post your friends' most recent scores and any free items they've won—or even beg you to play the game yourself. Posts from Facebook's social games typically include an image from the game and information about your friend's recent play. Click the image or button to sign up or play.

- **Facebook-generated content:** In addition to the posts you see from your friends, you'll also find some Facebook-generated content in your News Feed. Facebook likes to remind you of what you've posted and encourages you to share your memories. These posts are most often fun trips down memory lane—based on what you've posted to the Facebook site. In addition, Facebook aggressively suggests new people you might like to friend. These are typically friends of your existing friends, and Facebook really, really wants you to make them your friends, too. You can simply ignore these suggestions, tap or click Add Friend to add this person as a friend, or (if you have this option) tap or click Remove to have Facebook stop suggesting this person. (It won't stop Facebook from suggesting others, however!)

Hide Unwanted Posts

If these types of posts annoy you, you can choose to hide them in your News Feed. From the Facebook website, mouse over the post, click the down arrow at the top-right corner, and then click Hide All from This Game.

It's Not All Good

Think Before You Click

Facebook is like any community—there are always a few charlatans around to trick the naïve or unsuspecting. Beware links that seem too good to be true, such as ads for free iPads, unnecessary PC tune-ups, and the like. Facebook tries to keep these kinds of posts off the site but isn't always successful. So, think twice before you click—and if it smells fishy, don't click at all!

Viewing Your Friends' Stories

Facebook's mobile app now lets users collate selected posts into what they call a Story. A Facebook Story is a collection of photos and videos that combine to tell a story, at least in theory. (This is based on a similar feature in the competing Snapchat app that your grandkids probably use.)

Play a Story

If one of your Facebook friends has created a Story, you'll see it listed in the Stories bar at the top of the Facebook mobile app or in the right column on the Facebook website. Stories disappear 24 hours after creation.

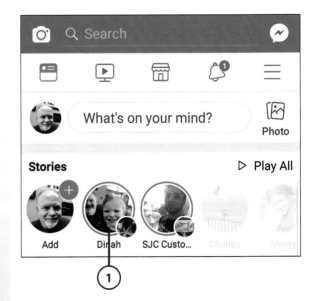

1. In the mobile app, go to the Stories bar at the top of the News Feed and tap the Story you want to view. (Alternatively, tap Play All to play all available Stories, one after another.) On the Facebook website, available Stories are displayed at the top of the right-hand column.

2. The Story now opens full-screen. Pictures and videos in the Story are displayed one at a time for a few seconds. Tap or click a picture to pause the playback.

3. The next Story plays automatically at the end of the current Story. Or, if you're in the mobile app, swipe right-to-left to view the next Story, or left-to-right to view the previous Story.

4. Tap or click the X to close the Story and return to the News Feed.

Viewing a Friend's Profile

If you want to see more of what a friend's been up to, you can view the person's profile page. A friend's profile includes detailed information about that friend, all that person's photos and videos, a list of that friend's friends, and all that friend's Facebook posts.

Explore a Profile

To display a friend's profile page, click or tap that person's name anywhere on the Facebook site. You can also enter the friend's name into the Facebook search box at the top of the News Feed and select that person's name from the search results.

(1) Basic information about the friend is displayed at the top of the profile page. You also see your own connections to that person—click or tap Friends to change your friend status, or click or tap Following or See First to change how you follow this person's posts. (This icon changes depending on what you've previously selected.)

(2) Tap or click About to view information about your friend—where she went to school, where she's lived, her contact info, her birthday, her relationship status, and more. (You'll only see the information your friend has entered and made public.)

(3) Tap or click Photos to view all the photos your friend has uploaded to Facebook.

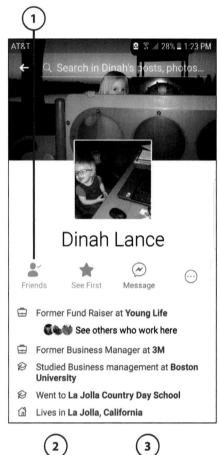

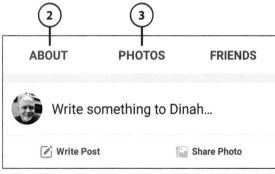

4 Tap or click Friends to view all your friend's other friends.

5 Tap or click within the Write Something To… box to write a public post to your friend.

6 Scroll to the Posts section to view all status updates posted by your friend.

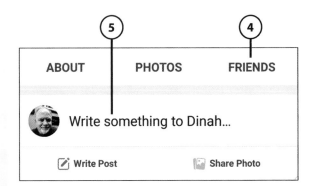

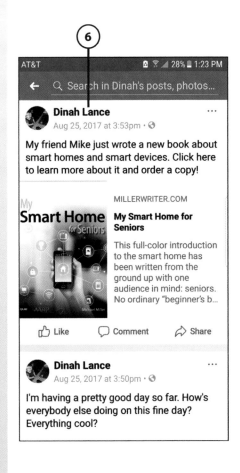

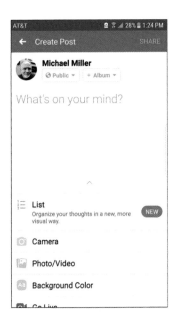

Updating Friends and Family on Your Activities

To let your family and friends know what you've been doing and thinking about, you need to post what Facebook calls a *status update*. Every status update you make is broadcast to everyone on your friends list, displayed in the News Feed on their home pages.

Updating Your Status

A status update is, at its most basic, a brief text message. It can be as short as a word or two, or it can be several paragraphs long; that's up to you. (Facebook lets you post updates with more than 60,000 characters, which should be more than long enough for most of us.)

Although a basic status update is all text, you can also attach other items to your status updates, including digital photographs, videos, and links to other web pages. You can also "tag" other Facebook users and groups in your updates so that their names appear as clickable links to their profile pages.

Tags

A *tag* is a way to mention other Facebook users in your status updates and photos. When a person is tagged in a post, the post appears in that person's Facebook feed, so he knows you're talking about him. In addition, readers can click a tagged name to display that person's profile page.

Post a Status Update

You can post a status update from the Facebook mobile app or on the Facebook website. It's just as easy either way.

(1) From the News Feed screen, click or tap within the Publisher (What's on Your Mind?) box.

(2) On the Facebook website, the Publisher box expands into a Make Post panel.

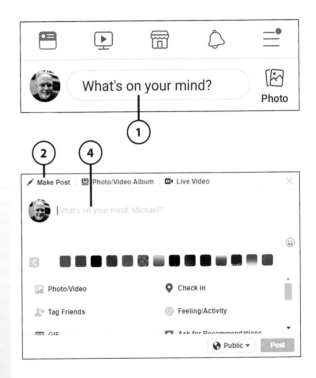

3 In the mobile app, the Create Post page is displayed.

4 Enter the text of your post into the What's on Your Mind? field.

5 If your post is relatively short and includes no other elements (photos, links, and so on), it appears with large text against a color or graphic background. Click or tap to select a background. (If you don't select a background color, the post defaults to normal black text on a white background.)

6 Tap Share (or click Post on the website) when done.

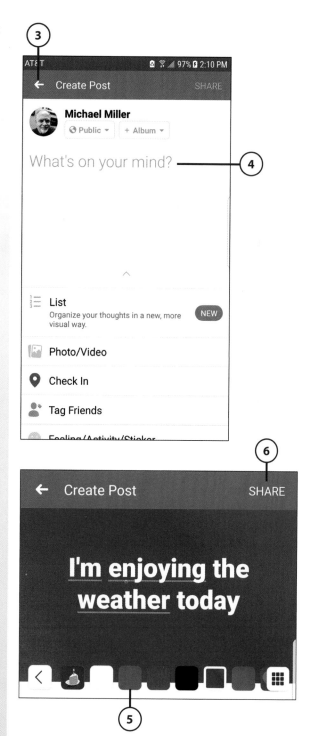

7 You may now be prompted to share to your News Feed and/ or Your Story. (They're not mutu- ally exclusive; you can do both.) Select News Feed to post this update to your News Feed.

8 To share this post to Your Story, select Your Story. This post in Your Story is visible to your friends for 24 hours.

9 Tap Share Now.

Share To

News Feed
Posts also show up on your timeline and in search results.
Share with: **Public** ▾

Your Story
Visible for 24 hours to:
Friends and Connections ▾

SHARE NOW

Your Story

Your Story is a newish feature based on a similar feature in the Instagram photo-sharing app. Your Story is simply a short-term collection of photos, videos, and text messages that your friends can view as a kind of slideshow. A post in Your Story is visible for just 24 hours, and then it disappears. Note that you can post a status update to both your News Feed (where it remains forever) and Your Story; News Feed, of course, is the default.

>>>Go Further
HASHTAGS

Facebook offers the option of including *hashtags* in your status updates. A hashtag is like a keyword, a word, or a phrase that describes the content of your post—and that readers can click to see similar posts with the same hashtag. A hashtag starts with the hash (#) character, followed by the keyword or phrase (with no spaces between the words). So, for example, a hashtag about this book might look like this: #MyFacebook. If you see a hashtag in a friend's status update, you can click it to display a list of other posts that include the same hashtag.

Post a Link to a Web Page

You can include links to other web pages in your status updates. Facebook adds a link to the specified page, and it also lets you include a thumbnail image from that page with the status update.

1. Start a new post as normal and enter any accompanying text.

2. Enter the URL (web address) for the page you want to link to as part of your update.

3. Facebook should recognize the link and might display an image from the website. (If a site has multiple images, you see left and right arrows at the top-left corner of the image. Click these arrows to select one of multiple images to accompany the link.)

4. Tap Share or click Post when done.

Delete the URL

If you don't want to display the web page's URL in the body of your status update, you can delete the address after the accompanying image is displayed. The link and accompanying image still display under your status update even after you delete the web page URL from your text.

Post a Photo or Video

Facebook enables you to embed digital photographs and videos in your posts. It's the Facebook equivalent of attaching a file to an email message.

1. On the Facebook website, go to the Publisher box and click Photo/Video Album to display the Open dialog box. *Or…*

2. In the Facebook mobile app, tap Photo to display your device's photo gallery.

3. Navigate to and select the photo or video file(s) you want to upload. You can upload a single video file or multiple photo files. (Tap to select multiple photos on your phone or tablet; to select more than one file on your computer, hold down the Ctrl key while you click each filename.)

4. Click Open or tap Done.

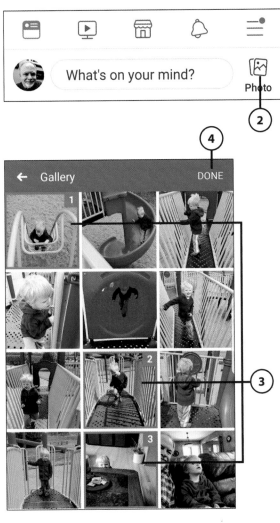

5 You're returned to the Publisher box or screen with your photo(s) added. Click or tap to add your location or another photo, if you want.

6 If you like, enter a short text message describing the photo(s) or video.

7 Tap Share or click Post.

Add Your Location to a Post

Facebook enables you to identify your current location in any post you make. This lets your friends know where you are at any given time.

1 Enter the text of your status update into the Publisher box as normal or select any photos you want to post.

2 Click or tap Check In.

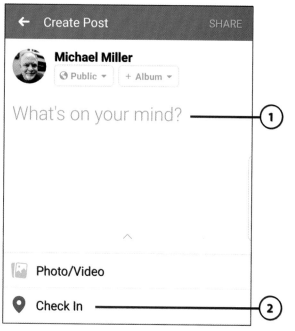

(**3**) If Facebook can tell your location automatically, it displays a list of options. Click or tap to select your current location.

(**4**) If Facebook doesn't display your current location, start entering your location manually; as you type, you see a list of suggested locations.

(**5**) Click or tap the correct location from the resulting list.

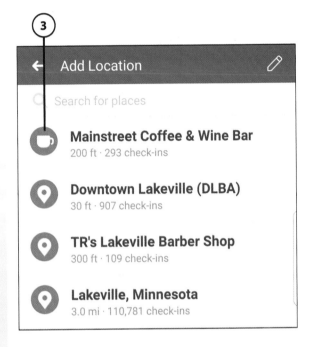

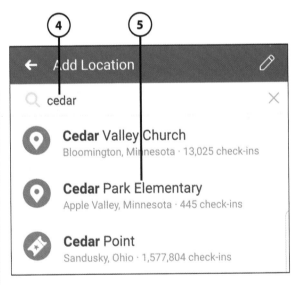

6 The location is added to your status update—and, in some instances, a map of the location is displayed. Click Post or tap Share to post the update.

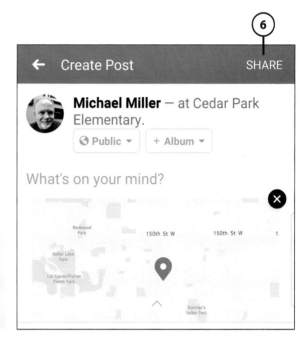

It's Not All Good

Don't Publicize Your Location

You might not want to identify your location on every post you make. If you post while you're away from home, you're letting potential burglars know that your house is empty. You're also telling potential stalkers where they can find you. For these reasons, use caution when posting your location in your status updates.

Tag a Friend in a Post

Sometimes you might want to mention one of your friends in a status update or include a friend who was with you when the post was made. You can do this by "tagging" friends in your status updates; the resulting post includes a link to the tagged person or persons.

(1) Enter the text of your status update into the Publisher box as normal or add any photos you want to post.

(2) Click or tap Tag Friends.

(3) In the mobile app, Facebook suggests friends you might want to tag. If your friends are listed here, tap their names.

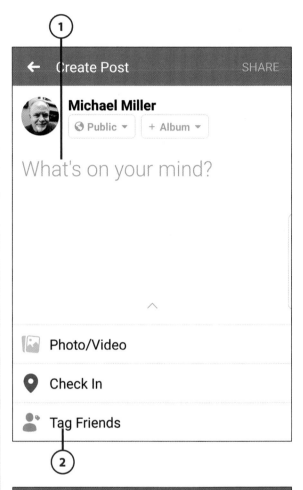

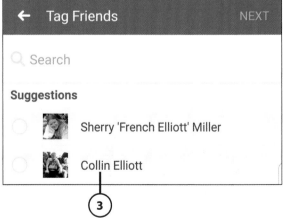

4 If your friend isn't listed, or if you're using the Facebook website, enter his or her name. As you type, Facebook displays a list with matching names from your Facebook friends list.

5 Click or tap your friend's name from the list.

6 Click or tap Next.

7 Your friend is now tagged in your post. Click Post or tap Share to post the update.

Tagged Friends

Clicking a tagged person's name in a status update displays that person's profile page.

Tell Friends What You're Doing—or How You're Feeling

Given the huge number of posts in which people write about what they're doing at the moment, Facebook has added a What Are You Doing? option to its status updates. This provides a very quick way to tell your friends what you're doing.

1 Enter the text of your status update into the Publisher box as normal. (Or, if you're just posting what you're doing, leave the Publisher box empty.)

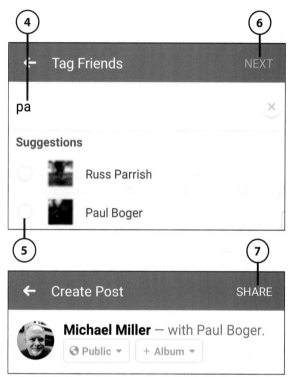

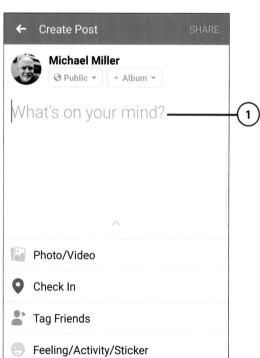

2   Click Feeling/Activity on the Facebook website, or tap Feeling/Activity/Sticker in the mobile app.

3   Tap Feelings (or click Feelings on the website) to add a feeling emoji.

4   Tap or click the feeling you want to express. *Or…*

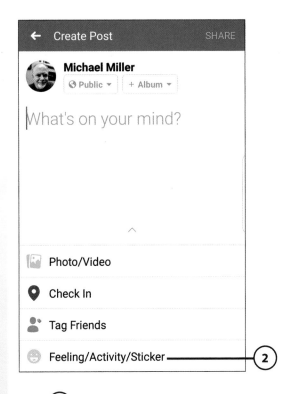

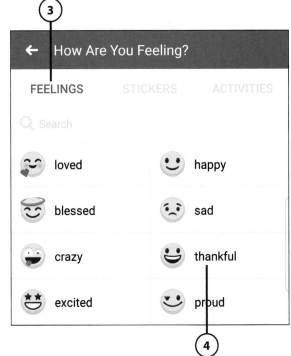

⑤ In the mobile app, tap Activities to display a list of activities. (On the website, activities are listed beneath the Feeling option.)

⑥ Tap or click the type of activity in which you are presently engaging.

⑦ Select the appropriate option for what you're doing.

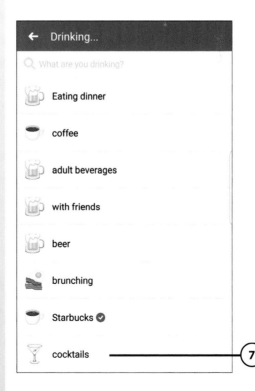

8 Your feeling or action is added to your post. Finish the rest of your status update as usual, and then click or tap Post or Share.

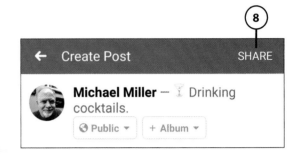

Insert an Emoji

An emoji is a small image or icon used to express an emotion or idea. You can insert emoji directly into the text of your Facebook status update.

1 Start entering the text of your message into the Publisher box.

2 On your mobile device, tap the Emoji icon on your onscreen keyboard.

3 On the Facebook website, click the Emoji icon.

④ Tap or click the type of emoji you'd like to browse.

⑤ Tap or click to insert a specific emoji. (You can insert more than one, if you like.)

⑥ The emoji is inserted into the text of your status update. Click or tap Share or Post to post the update.

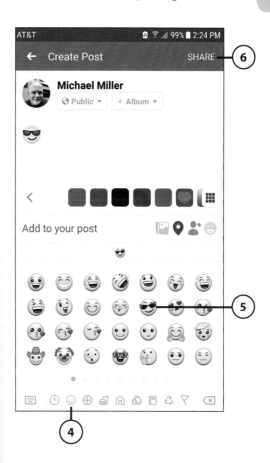

Add a GIF

Facebook also lets you add GIFs—larger animated images, often short clips from movies or TV shows. The GIF you select is added like a photo to your status update.

① Start a status update as normal and then tap or click GIF.

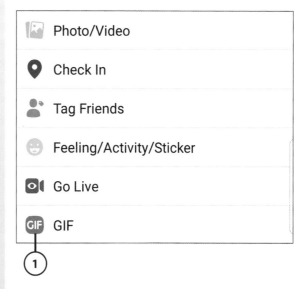

(2) Tap or click to select the GIF you want. (You can scroll through available GIFs, or search for a specific type of GIF, if you'd like.)

(3) The GIF is added to your status update. Click or tap Share or Post to post the update.

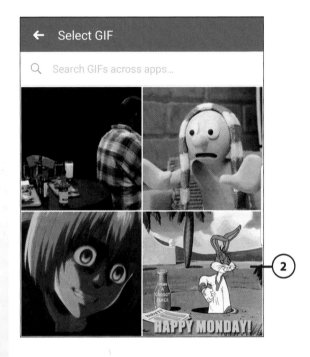

Add a Sticker

Facebook also lets you add stickers to your status updates. A sticker is like an emoji, sort of, but with more detailed artwork—just like a physical sticker in the real world.

(1) Start a new status update as normal and then, on your mobile device, tap Feeling/Activity/ Sticker—or, on the Facebook website, click Sticker.

(2) In the mobile app, tap Stickers.

(3) Tap or click the type of sticker you want.

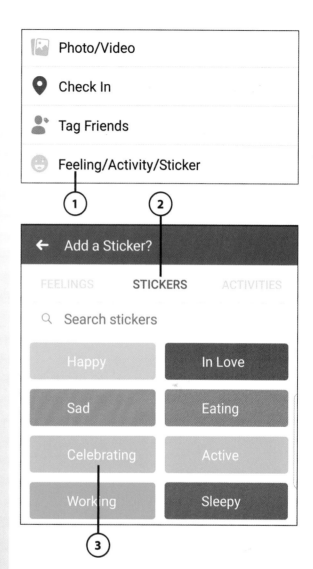

(4) Scroll through or search for a specific sticker, and then tap or click the sticker you want.

(5) The sticker is added to your status update, like a photo. Tap or click Share or Post to post the update.

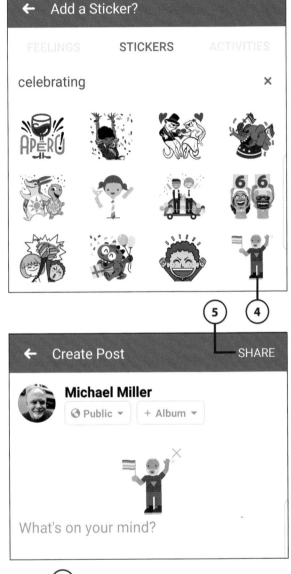

Ask for Recommendations

Looking for a plumber? Or a nice restaurant? Or maybe a recommendation for a babysitter or dog walker or handyman? Whatever you're looking for, chances are one of your Facebook friends will have a recommendation. All you have to do is ask.

(1) Start a status update as normal and then tap or click Ask for Recommendations.

2 In the mobile app, tap Add a Location and select where you're looking.

3 On the Facebook website, click within Where Are You Looking for Recommendations and select a location.

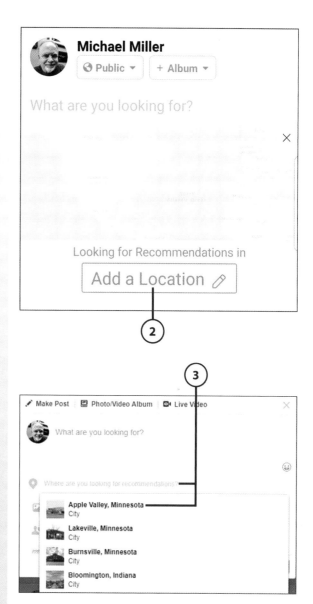

(**4**) Enter the text of your status update—what you're looking for.

(**5**) Click or tap Share or Post to post your request.

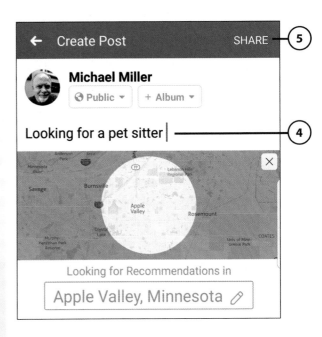

Start a Poll

You can also use Facebook to poll your friends about a given topic. It'll be a decidedly unscientific poll, but you'll get a good idea of what your friends are thinking.

(**1**) Start a status update as normal and then tap or click Poll.

(**2**) Enter the question you want answered into the Ask a Question box.

(**3**) Enter the first possible answer into the Option 1 box.

(**4**) Enter the second possible answer into the Option 2 box.

(**5**) Tap or click the Poll Ends box and select the end time for your poll—1 Day, 1 Week, Never, or Custom.

(**6**) Click Post or tap Share to post your poll.

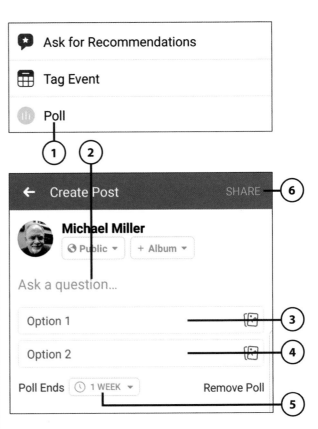

Post a List

Facebook makes it easy for you to create list-based status updates. You can choose from popular list topics, such as "Songs I can't stop listening to" or "Things I need to get done," or create your own custom lists.

(1) Create a status update as normal and then tap or click List.

(2) Select one of the list topics listed and proceed to step 5. *Or…*

(3) Tap or click Create New to create a custom list.

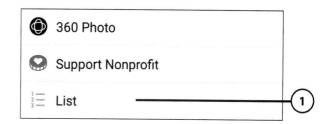

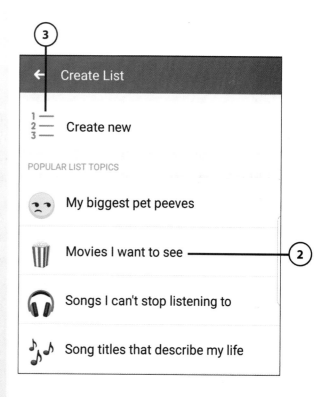

(4) Tap or click the Title field and enter a title for this list.

(5) Tap or click the first Add an Item field and add the first list item.

(6) Tap or click Add Another Item to add another item for the list. Repeat this step until your list is completed.

(7) Select whether you want a numbered or bulleted list.

(8) Tap the background color you want for this list.

(9) Enter optional information about this list into the Say Something About This List field.

(10) Tap Share or click Post to post this list.

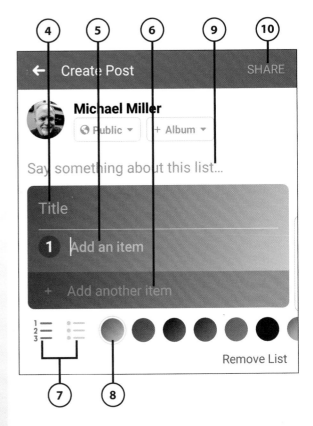

Support a Nonprofit

If you have a nonprofit organization you support, you can solicit donations to this cause from your Facebook friends.

(1) Start a new status update as normal and then tap or click Support Nonprofit.

2 Select a nonprofit from those listed, or search for one.

3 Enter why you want people to donate to this cause.

4 Tap Share or click Post to post this donation request. When your friends read this post, they can click or tap the Donate button to make a donation.

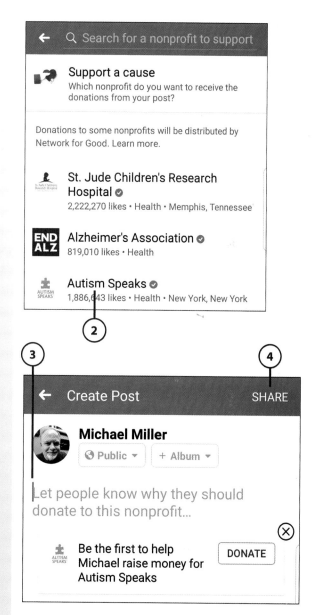

Determine Who Can—or Can't—See a Status Update

By default, the updates you post to Facebook can be seen by everyone on your friends list. If you'd rather send a given post to a more select group of people, or to everyone on the site, you can change the privacy settings for an individual post. This enables only selected people to see that post; other people on your friends list won't see it at all.

(1) Enter the text of your status update, or any photos you want to upload, into the Publisher box as normal.

(2) Click or tap the Privacy button or arrow to display a list of privacy options.

(3) Select Public to let everyone on Facebook see the post.

(4) Select Friends to make a post visible only to people on your friends list.

(5) Select Friends Except and then select specific people or groups who you don't want to see the post.

(6) Click See More on your mobile device (or More on the Facebook website) to view more privacy options.

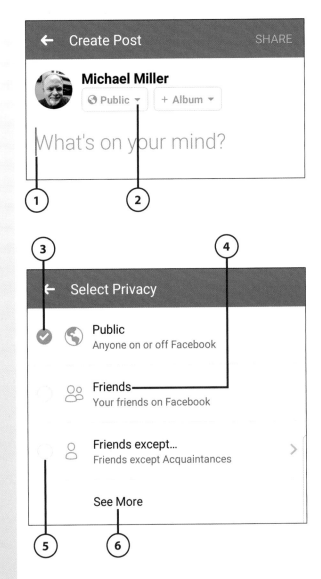

7 Select Specific Friends to only show this post to those friends you select.

8 Select Only Me to hide this post from everyone except yourself.

9 Select See All to share this post with a specific list of individuals.

10 Back in your post, click Post or tap Share to send this status update to those people you've selected.

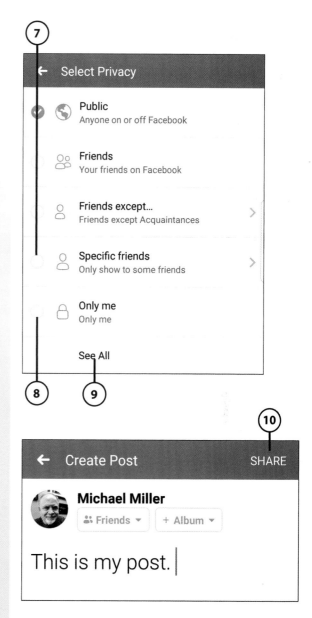

>>>Go Further

POSTING ETIQUETTE

Writing a Facebook status update is a bit like sending a text message on your cell phone. As such, status updates do not have to—and often don't—conform to proper grammar, spelling, and sentence structure. It's common to abbreviate longer words, use familiar acronyms, substitute single letters and numbers for whole words, and refrain from all punctuation.

Then there's the issue of how often you should update your Facebook status. Unfortunately, there are no hard and fast rules as to posting frequency. Some people post once a week, others post daily, others post several times a day. In general, you should post when you have something interesting to share—and not because you feel obligated to make a post.

Posting Content from Other Websites

Facebook is all about sharing things with your friends. Naturally, you can share your thoughts and activities via status updates; you can also upload and share your personal photos and videos.

But Facebook is also connected to many other sites on the Web. This enables you to share content you find elsewhere with your Facebook friends. It's all about posting content from other websites to your Facebook Timeline—and your friends' News Feeds.

Share Content from Another Site

Many websites would like you to share their content with your friends on Facebook. When you're browsing another site and find something interesting to share, look for a Facebook button. This button is sometimes included in a special "sharing" section of the page; it's often labeled Facebook, Facebook Share, Facebook Like, or Facebook Recommend.

News Sharing

Facebook sharing buttons are especially common on news-type sites, which makes it easy to share the articles you find there.

1 Click or tap the Facebook button on the other website. (If you're currently signed into your Facebook account, you probably won't need to log in again. However, if you're prompted to sign into your Facebook account at this point, enter your email address and password, and then click or tap the Log In button.)

2 What you see next depends on the site. In some instances, the link to the page is posted automatically without any comments from you. In other instances, you have the option of including a personal comment with the link; enter your comment if you like.

3 Click or tap the Share, Share Link, or Post button, depending on what you see.

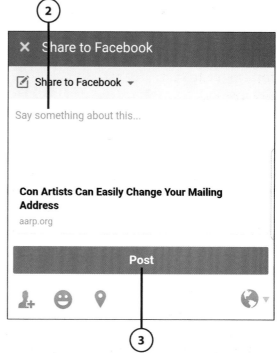

Dinah Lance
2 mins · 🌐

Granddaughter Hayley was in the church musical this weekend. She was great!

Dinah Lance
Just now · 🌐

Good news -- Oliver is out of the hospital and recuperating from his recent surgery. Send him lots of good-well messages!

👍 Like   💬 Comment   ↪ Share

In this chapter, you discover the types of things you should share on Facebook—and those you shouldn't.

→ What's Good to Post on Facebook
→ What *Not* to Post on Facebook
→ Learning Facebook Etiquette

What to Post—and What *Not* to Post—on Facebook

Facebook is not your own private diary or soapbox. It's a public website, where what you post is visible to all your friends and family—and, potentially, millions of other users. (And once you've posted it, it's online forever!)

As such, it's important to make your posts interesting to the people who'll be reading them. It's also important not to post certain types of information; with everyone you know—or may know in the future—reading everything you post, it's easy to get yourself in trouble with a few taps of the computer keyboard.

What's Good to Post on Facebook

If you've been on Facebook for any time at all, you've seen your share of boring, self-indulgent, and useless status updates from friends. Not everyone has the knack for posting updates that you really want to read.

It's important to post interesting status updates. But what, exactly, qualifies as something worthwhile to post about?

Post Interesting Information

The best advice I can give for what to post on Facebook is anything that your friends and family are likely to find interesting. Not things you might find interesting, but what others might find interesting about you.

Interesting Topics

To make sure your updates get read, focus on interesting and unique topics. The fact that you went to a concert or read a good book is interesting; that you woke up with a headache or just had a cup of tea is not.

(1) Post things you want to share with your Facebook friends. These are moments and events that are not only important to you, but also are things you think your friends might care about, too.

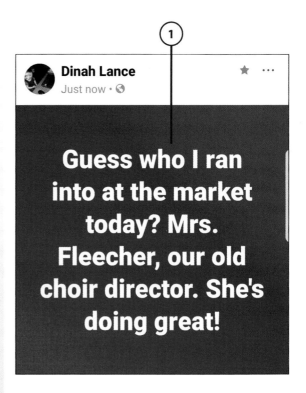

2 Post things that your friends and family want to know about. Friends typically want to know if you've done or seen something interesting, taken a vacation, met a mutual friend, and such. If you think someone's interested in it, post it.

3 Post about major life events—things in your life that your friends and family *need* to know about. These are important moments and events, such as anniversaries, birthdays, and celebrations.

2

Dinah Lance
Just now •

Had a great vacation last week. Good to be back, but really hated to leave.

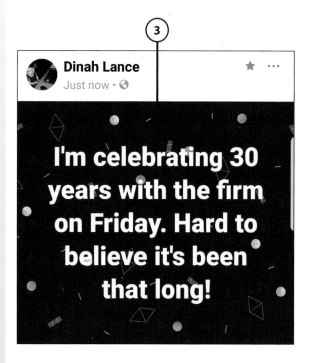

3

Dinah Lance
Just now •

I'm celebrating 30 years with the firm on Friday. Hard to believe it's been that long!

(4) Post interesting thoughts. Share your wisdom with your friends and family via Facebook status updates—in a noncontroversial, inoffensive way, if you can.

Get Permission First

Before you post something about your spouse, a family member, or a friend, get that person's permission. Some people would rather you not share their information with the Facebook universe.

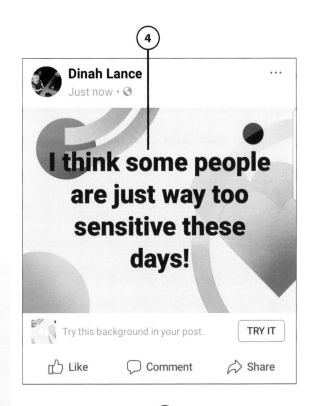

Post Important Information

Many people use Facebook as a kind of bulletin board for their families and friends. One post can inform many people about something important; it's a lot more efficient than sending out dozens of emails or making tons of phone calls. Again—for privacy reasons, be cautious about what you share and with whom.

(1) Post if something has happened to you. If you've been ill or hospitalized, gotten a new job, moved to a new town, or whatever, use Facebook to let everyone know about it.

(2) Post if something has happened to your spouse or partner. Many of your friends are likely mutual friends, so if anything major has happened, include that information in your status update—especially if your spouse or partner can't post, for whatever reason.

(3) Post if something has happened to another family member. You might know something about a cousin or nephew that others in your family might not know about. Share your information with other family members via a Facebook post.

(4) Post if something has happened to a mutual friend. It's tough to keep track of all your old friends. Start the chain going by posting what you know, and let your other friends pass it on to their friends, too.

What *Not* to Post on Facebook

There are some things you probably shouldn't post on Facebook. Many of the posts you see from friends are mundane and uninteresting; some are inflammatory and offensive. And then there are those posts that just contain too much information about personal matters you'd rather not know.

It's important, then, to think before you post. Remember that Facebook is not a private diary; it's a public website with more than 2 billion users. Some things simply shouldn't be shared with all those people.

Avoid Uninteresting or Unwise Posts

By default, all your Facebook friends will see everything you post. Post only that information that you'd want your friends (or spouse or grandkids) to read.

- Don't complain. The last thing your Facebook friends want to find in their News Feeds is your private griping. It's okay to grouse and be grumpy from time to time (you're entitled), but don't use Facebook as your personal forum for petty grievances. If you have a personal problem, deal with it; whining gets old really fast. (We especially don't want to hear if you're having a fight with your partner or problems with your kids. This sort of thing is best kept private.)

- Don't post confessions. Facebook is not the place to come clean about past indiscretions; it's a public forum, not a private confessional. If you need to confess something to someone, do it in a more private way.

- Don't get too personal. Facebook is definitely not the best place to share intimate details about your life. Most people feel a little awkward when someone discloses just a little too much about his or her personal life. A good rule of thumb is that if you don't want your kids or grandkids to know about it, don't share it on Facebook.

- Don't post anything that anyone—including lawyers, employers, or the police—could use against you. When you post a status update, it's there for everyone to see, friend or foe. It gets back to that confessional thing; if you think something could come back to bite you, don't post it.

- Don't post embarrassing photos of yourself or others, and don't tag anyone else who might be in those photos—especially your children or grandchildren. You don't want to humiliate yourself or your family online.

- Don't post just to get attention. Some people do what we call *vaguebooking,* which is the practice of posting a message that's intentionally vague but hints at some personal problem or crisis (such as "Life is so unfair. You know who I'm talking about."). People vaguebook to get their friends to respond with worried inquiries about what's wrong; it's highly manipulative and sure to create enmity over time. If you really have some sort of problem, it's better to call a friend instead of posting about it publicly to everyone on Facebook.

- Don't post if you don't have anything interesting to say. Posting too many meaningless updates will cause friends to start ignoring everything you post.

Avoid Posting Personal Information

There's a whole other class of information you shouldn't post on Facebook—personal information that could be used by identity thieves to hijack your bank accounts or site memberships online. If you don't want to become a victim of identity theft, avoid posting too many personal details to your Facebook account.

- *Don't* post your personal contact information—phone number, street address, email address, and so forth. (And edit your profile so that this contact info is private, not public.) You don't want complete strangers to contact or harass you.

- *Don't* post location information when you're away from home. This can tip off burglars that your house is empty or notify stalkers where you can be found. Wait until after you get home to share where you had dinner or vacationed.

- *Don't* post the layout of your house. You don't want to give potential burglars a roadmap to all your goodies.

- *Don't* post your Social Security number (SSN). Ever. If your SSN gets in the wrong hands, identity theft will result.

- *Don't* post other pieces of information that could be used to gain access to your online accounts—your birthdate, birthplace, mother's maiden name, first pet, and so forth. This information is typically used for "challenge questions" if you forget your password on a website; if you post this information where potential thieves can see it, they might be able to reset your password and gain access to your online accounts.

Learning Facebook Etiquette

Your status updates on Facebook should be not only interesting but also easy to read. Not that each post must be letter perfect, but there are some guidelines you should follow.

Carefully Compose Your Status Updates

Facebook status updates are not long, thought-out missives. A status update is more immediate than an email and less well constructed than a handwritten letter.

That said, more people will read your posts if you follow some simple guidelines. Your status updates don't have to be perfect, but they do need to be in the ballpark.

- Be personal and personable. Your writing on Facebook should be light and informal, not stiff and professional. Write as you'd talk, in your own personal voice. Make it sound like you—and be as friendly as you know how to be.

- Keep your posts short. Facebook users, even your dear childhood friends, don't have the attention span, the patience, or the inclination to read long tomes. They want quick bits of information, something they can scan without necessarily reading. Keep each status update to a paragraph, no more than a few sentences—and the shorter the better.

- Include links and photos in your posts. A Facebook status update doesn't have to be just text. You can—and should—include photos and links to other websites in your posts. In fact, most posts today have some sort of visual element. There's nothing wrong with text-only posts; it's just that users are drawn to—and tend to expect—more visually interesting posts. This means that people are more likely to ignore text-only posts in favor of posts with some sort of image. If you can illustrate your point with a photo, or a link to a picture on another web page, then do so.

Know the Shorthand

As anyone of a younger generation will no doubt attest, writing a Facebook status update is a bit like sending a text message on your cell phone. You do it quickly, without a lot of preparation or editing. It's an in-the-moment communication, and as such you can't be expected to take the time to create a grammatically perfect message.

For this reason, Facebook status updates do not have to—and seldom do—conform to proper grammar, spelling, and sentence structure. It's common to abbreviate longer words, use familiar acronyms, substitute single letters and numbers for whole words, and refrain from all punctuation.

For example, instead of spelling out the word "Friday," you can just write "Fri." Instead of saying "See you later," just say "later." Instead of spelling out "New York City," use the abbreviation "NYC."

Misspellings

It's also acceptable, at least to some users, to have the occasional misspelling. It's not something I personally like to do or see, but I'm a professional writer and pickier about these things than many people; most people will let it slide if you get the spelling or grammar wrong once in a while.

Younger users, especially, like to use a sort of online shorthand (or "Facebook grammar") to pack as much as possible into a short status update. These are the same acronyms and abbreviations that have been used for decades in text messaging, instant messaging, and Internet chat rooms. You might not be familiar with this shorthand, much of which is detailed in Table 7.1. It may be a tad unseemly for older folks to use this hip lingo, but it certainly helps to know what everything means when you're reading posts from your kids or grandkids.

Table 7.1 Common Facebook Acronyms

Acronym	Description
AF	As f**k (as in, "angry as f**k" or "cool as f**k")
AFAIK	As far as I know
ASAP	As soon as possible
ASL	Age/sex/location
B/W	Between
B4	Before
BAE	Before anyone else
BC	Because
BFN	Bye for now
BR	Best regards
BRB	Be right back
BTW	By the way
CU	See you
Cuz	Because
DAE	Does anyone else
EOD	End of discussion
FB	Facebook
FBF	Flashback Friday
FTF	Face to face

Acronym	Description
FTFY	Fixed that for you
FWIW	For what it's worth
FYI	For your information
GM	Good morning
GN	Good night
GTR	Getting ready
HMU	Hit me up
HTH	Hope that helps
IDK	I don't know
IM	Instant message
IMHO	In my humble opinion
IRL	In real life
JK	Just kidding
JSYK	Just so you know
K	Okay
L8	Late
L8r	Later
LMAO	Laughing my ass off
LMK	Let me know
LOL	Laughing out loud
NSFW	Not safe for work
OH	Overheard
OMG	Oh my God
OT	Off topic
OTOH	On the other hand
Pls *or* Plz	Please

Acronym	Description
Ppl *or* peeps	People
R	Are
Rly	Really
ROFL	Rolling on the floor laughing
SD	Sweet dreams
SMH	Shaking my head
TBH	To be honest
TBT	Throwback Thursday
Tht	That
Thx *or* Tnx	Thanks
TIL	Today I learned
TL;DR	Too long; didn't read
TY	Thank you
TTYL	Talk to you later
U	You
Ur	Your
WFM	Works for me
WTF	What the f**k
WTH	What the hell
YMMV	Your mileage may vary
YSK	You should know
YW	You're welcome
Zzz	Sleeping

>>>Go Further

HOW OFTEN SHOULD YOU POST?

How often should you update your Facebook status? That's an interesting question, without a defined answer.

Some of my Facebook friends post frequently—several times a day. Some only post occasionally, once a month or so. Most, however, post once a day or once every few days. So, if there's an average, that's it.

Some of the more frequent posters are justified, in that they post a lot of interesting information. Other frequent posters I find more annoying, in that their posts are more personal and less practical; every little tic and burp is immortalized in its own update. That's probably posting too much.

On the other hand, my friends who only post once a month or so probably aren't trying hard enough. I'd like to hear from them more often; certainly they're doing something interesting that's worth posting about. After a while, I tend to forget that they're still around.

So you need to post often enough that your friends don't forget about you, but not so often that they wish you'd just shut up. I suppose your update frequency has something to do with what it is you're doing and how interesting that is. But it's okay to post just to let people know you're still there—as long as you don't do so hourly.

Like Page   •••

February 16 · 🌐

Studies have shown that dandelions may be able to kill cancer cells. Read more here. #dandelions #study #preventcancer

FAKE!

Dandelion May Disintegrate Cancer In 48 Hours

Dandelions are loaded with calcium that is essential for the growth of bones and keeping them strong. They are also full of antioxidants like vitamin C and luteolin.

FITLIFE.TV

👍❤️😮 544   31 Comments   317 Shares

👍 Like   💬 Comment   ↪ Share

•••

June 24, 2016 · ☀

hahah -- The Onion nails it again.

FAKE!

Queen Elizabeth Screaming At Stockbroker To Dump Everything

LONDON—Following the United Kingdom's historic vote to exit the European Union, sources confirmed that Queen Elizabeth II spent Friday frantically screaming at her...

ONION.COM

👍😆 5   1 Share

👍 Like   💬 Comment   ↪ Share

In this chapter, you discover all the fake and phony stuff that's shared on Facebook—and learn how to distinguish between what's true and what's false in your News Feed.

Dealing with Fake News and Other Questionable Stuff

No doubt you've seen them in your News Feed: posts, memes, and links to stories that make claims that don't feel quite right. Maybe it's something about the behavior of a given politician, or the details of some supposed new law, or even some wild claim that sounds more like a conspiracy theory than a news headline.

Chances are that what you're seeing isn't factual. It's what some people call "fake news"—a bunch of lies and hoaxes designed to rile up the uninformed and easily influenced. And, if you're not careful, you can easily be duped by the latest round of falsehoods circulating on Facebook—perhaps by some of your best Facebook friends.

Understanding Fake News

Fake news is just what it says it is—a news headline or article that purports to be real but isn't. It's made-up news, stories that are more fiction than fact. It's stuff you may want to believe but shouldn't.

People have been making stuff up forever, in the form of misleading stories, lies, hoaxes, and propaganda. It's just that this sort of thing spreads faster today. It used to be that this sort of misinformation would be spread by word of mouth; a friend would tell another friend about some supposed thing happening, and then that friend would tell somebody else, and eventually you'd hear about it. It took some time for the rumors and such to make their way throughout even a small community.

Today, however, all someone has to do is post the latest piece of misinformation on Facebook, and literally seconds later it can spread around the entire planet. One influential person posts an ill-informed link to a fake news story, and hundreds of people read that story in their News Feeds—and take it as the gospel truth. It gets even worse when some of these people pass on the original post to their Facebook friends, who share it with their friends, who share it with theirs; pretty soon millions of people worldwide are exposed to the misinformation, and the original falsehood takes on a life of its own that is now difficult to dispute.

Going Viral

When a piece of information (or video or other type of file) gets circulated around a large number of people, it's said to have gone *viral*. The term comes from the way a biological virus spreads; on the Internet, anything that gets passed from person to person in this fashion resembles biological viral behavior.

This is how fake news becomes a real issue. It's especially prevalent in the world of politics, but it can permeate rational discussion in all fields of interest.

A Few Examples...

When we say fake news, what exactly are we talking about? There are variations on the theme (which we'll discuss later in this chapter), but I'm mainly talking about made-up, phony news stories, the kind you used to read in the weekly tabloid papers in the check-out lanes at your local grocery store. Now those fake stories are posted on fake websites and then shared on Facebook and other social media.

What kinds of fake stories are we talking about? Well, here are some of the top fake news headlines shared on Facebook in 2017, in no certain order:

- "Elderly Woman Accused of Training Her 65 Cats to Steal from Neighbors"

- "Malia Obama Expelled from Harvard"

- "Morgan Freeman: 'Jailing Hillary' Best Way To 'Restore Public Faith In Govt'"

- "Morgue Employee Cremated by Mistake While Taking a Nap"

- "NPR: 25 Million Votes for Clinton Completely Fake"

- "Ohio Cemetery Exhuming Bodies of Confederate Soldiers"

- "President Trump Orders the Execution of Five Turkeys Pardoned by Obama"

- "Russian Scientists Discover Cure for Homosexuality"

All of these stories were totally fake. Not a drop of truth in any of them (which means if you saw and believed any of them, you got taken).

Let's look at one such fake story in more detail. During the 2016 presidential election, a white supremacist Twitter account made the claim that the New York City Police Department had discovered the existence of a human-trafficking ring operating out of a Washington, DC-based pizzeria named Comet Ping Pong. This ring was supposedly tied to Democratic presidential candidate Hillary Clinton and her chief of staff, John Podesta.

This claim was, of course, totally fabricated. Although there is a pizza joint in Washington named Comet Ping Pong, it is not the headquarters for any human-trafficking operations, and Clinton and Podesta are not tied to the pizza parlor or any such unsavory operations.

The truth of the matter didn't stop the original tweet from being passed around online from person to person and eventually being picked up by multiple right-wing message boards and Facebook feeds. It even got top billing on many so-called fake news websites, which helped the unfounded rumor to spread even further and faster.

Before long, "Pizzagate," as the ruckus was ultimately dubbed, had to be addressed in the mainstream media. Many unwitting individuals believed what they heard and took to harassing the owners and staff of Comet Ping Pong online and in person. One such true believer even took it upon himself to personally visit the pizza place and fire off three rounds from an AR-15-style assault rifle. (He was arrested for that.)

And all this happened because one person posted online something totally fabricated. That's how fake news and innuendo spread and become truly dangerous online.

And a Few More...

The Pizzagate situation is just one (very prominent) example of fake news and how it impacts people in the real world. There are hundreds of other examples that I could cite, many of them political in nature, but many more related to other hot- and not-so-hot-button topics. Fake news sites have sprung up to muddy the waters about climate change, vaccinations and autism, genetically modified food, gun violence, space travel, racial issues, you name it. (And that's not counting the almost constant barrage of UFO and Bigfoot conspiracy theory sites....)

Politics and Fake News

Perhaps not unsurprisingly, almost half (23 of the top 50) fake news stories on Facebook last year were political in nature. (Politics always seems to bring out the worst in some people.)

On the surface, much of this fake news is relatively harmless. (I mean, Bigfoot? Seriously?) But some of this false information could be deadly.

Take, for example, the topic of fake medical news. Yes, there are websites dispensing bogus medical advice, oftentimes pushing naturopathic and alternative cures in lieu of proven medical solutions. Fake news stories emanating from these sites have oozed across the Internet in recent years, many promising miracle cures that the medical establishment is, for some reason, hiding from the public.

If you've been on Facebook for any length of time, you've probably seen a few of these articles. Some of the more popular articles purport to offer a true cure for cancer, typically via some form of naturalistic treatment. One of my favorites has the headline, "Dandelion Weed Can Boost Your Immune System and Cure Cancer." Which, of course, it can't.

In every instance, the claims in these fake medical news articles have been discredited by doctors and healthcare researchers. Yet the fake stories persist, and people persist in reading and sometimes believing them.

This is not harmless folly. If you're a cancer victim and take these articles at face value, you might think you can stop your current expensive and often invasive treatments and switch to one of these holistic (and wholly disproven) solutions. Abandoning traditional medicine in favor of fake solutions can not only cost you the money for the fake meds, but it could literally result in death.

Recognizing Different Types of Fake News

So far, we've discussed "fake news" in very general terms. In reality, there are many different types of false information disseminated online, and not all for the same purpose or effect.

Fake News

Let's start with the most common type of fake news—literally fake news stories. At its most obvious, fake news is a news story that is deliberately false. These fake news stories are filled with lies and made-up "facts" about a particular topic. They describe events that didn't happen—or didn't happen the way the story describes.

In other words, fake news is fiction, in the form of a purportedly (but not really) real news article.

You will unfortunately find fake news stories, or links to them, in many of your friends' Facebook News Feeds. These links often point to stories on fake news websites that exist purely to disseminate fake news articles—hoaxes, disinformation, and propaganda. The stories posted on these websites then get shared via Facebook and other social media.

The intent of these fake news sites is to mislead people into thinking they're reading real news articles. They're neither satirical nor accidental. The writers are purposefully crafting believable-sounding but totally fraudulent articles, typically for their own financial or political gain. (These fraudsters make money by selling advertising on their fake news sites—and the more outrageous the fake stories, the more visitors they attract!)

Because of the outsized influence of these fake news sites, especially during the 2016 presidential election, many view this sort of propaganda as a threat to American democracy. If enough people believe the fake news, not only are voters misled but genuine news is delegitimized. It becomes more and more difficult for people to determine the real from the fake, and that shakes everything up.

Alternative Facts

Not all of the untruths spread online come from organized fake news sites. Some of what you read on Facebook and other social media are plain old lies—you know, when someone deliberately says something that isn't true.

For some reason, some people have trouble calling a lie a lie. In the mainstream media, you're more likely to hear that someone "misspoke" or told an "untruth" or "falsehood." Sometimes a person is said to have "distorted the facts." And some politicians now refer to their lies as "alternative facts."

Whatever you call it, a lie is a lie, and the person telling it is a liar. But what if a person doesn't tell the original lie; they just pass it on via a social media post? The person sharing the lie has the excuse that someone else said it, and he's just relating it without judgment. This might technically absolve the second person from the original sin, but passing on a lie as if it's the truth is just as good as lying, if you ask me.

In any case, be on the lookout for people lying or sharing lies on Facebook and other social media. Again, just because someone (even someone important) says something doesn't make it true. It may not technically be fake news, but it's just as false.

Conspiracy Theories

Conspiracy theories have been around as long as anyone can remember; some people want to believe that certain events are much more complex than we are led to believe. There are people who believe that JFK's assassination was part of a nefarious plot, or that the moon landing was faked, or that Elvis Presley faked his own death. Despite facts proving otherwise, these conspiracy theories persist.

In fact, conspiracy theorists have become more emboldened in recent years, thanks to others sharing their theories over the Internet. Facebook and other social media make it easier for those of like minds to pass their theories back and forth and to gain additional exposure to the previously uninitiated. If you haven't yet seen a particular conspiracy theory, it might look reasonable when you see it in a friend's News Feed.

Why do some people believe these wild claims? For some, it's a way of trying to make sense out of seemingly random events. It just doesn't make any sense that a lone gunman could slip through the cracks and shoot a president, so there has to be more to the story. Hence the creation of a conspiracy behind the whole thing; that's somehow more comforting than acknowledging that random events sometimes just happen.

In any case, Facebook is rife with conspiracy theories of all shapes and sizes. Don't believe them.

Propaganda

Some fake news is outright propaganda—information (or, more likely, disinformation) used to mislead or promote a particular point of view. Propaganda is particularly popular (and particularly potent) in politics, where one side spouts selective facts or blatant untruths in an effort to promote its cause or disparage the opposite side.

We're all targets of propaganda—from one or the other political parties, from our government, even from foreign governments. As noted previously, Russia has been accused of using propaganda to try to influence our country's elections by spreading disinformation about Democratic candidate Hillary Clinton on Facebook and other social media. China has built a multi-billion dollar media empire to spread pro-Communist propaganda around the globe. And some claim that the Qatar-based Al Jazeera television network is being used to spread Islamic propaganda throughout the Middle East and beyond.

The fact is, big players—political parties, governments, and movements—have always used propaganda to influence the masses and will undoubtedly continue to do so. What's changed is they're now doing it via Facebook and other social media.

Biased News

Listen to some people in the political sphere, and you're bound to hear that this or that particular news outlet is fake news. Although this can be the case, in most instances the person talking simply doesn't like the viewpoint espoused by that news outlet. That doesn't make the news from that outlet fake, but it could make it biased.

Let's be honest here. We live in a politically polarized society, where one side doesn't trust the other, and few want to work together for the common good. This polarized environment spreads to news outlets big and small, with those of a particular viewpoint claiming that media with a different view are biased and not to be believed.

It's true that some news media strike a bias to the liberal or conservative side of things. For example, it's fair to say that Fox News is somewhat biased in a conservative direction, whereas MSNBC holds somewhat of a liberal bias. (Compared to these two outlets, CNN lies somewhere in the middle.) This can be seen by the stories they choose to cover, the "experts" they choose to interview, even the slant they put on their coverage. That doesn't mean their coverage is fraudulent, just that it comes from a certain viewpoint.

Ideally, you know the political bias of a certain outlet and take that into account when reading something from it or watching it. It's good if you can avoid getting all your news from outlets that share the same bias; you want to get a variety of viewpoints to avoid creating your own echo chamber.

>>>Go Further
FINDING RELIABLE MEDIA

Although obvious biases exist, most mainstream media is more balanced than political die-hards would like to believe. Conservatives might rail against the "lamestream media" and liberals against the "corporate media," but most major national newspapers, magazines, and news channels are pretty accurate when it comes to reporting the daily news.

How do you know if a given news source is reliable? One good test is if the outlet employs some sort of ombudsman to listen to consumer complaints and offer in-house criticism. If a newspaper or news channel is open to self-examination and free to issue corrections when it's wrong, you're in good hands.

Let's put this more simply. If you want to get the straight news with minimal bias and opinion, go to the major broadcast networks (ABC, CBS, NBC, and PBS), the major national newspapers and news magazines (*The New York Times, The New Yorker, USA Today, The Wall Street Journal, The Washington Post*), and legitimate online news sites (*Politico*, Yahoo! News). Also good are the Associated Press, CNN, and Reuters. Major foreign news sources are also good, such as the BBC, *The Economist, The Guardian*.

So when it comes to straight news coverage, the mainstream media does a pretty good job. If you think all the major newspapers are lefty rags or conservative mouthpieces, chances are that it's your views that are biased, not the source's.

Opinions

When I was a youngster, our household watched the *CBS Evening News* with Walter Cronkite. Mr. Cronkite spoke with an authority and engendered a level of trust not seen in today's generation of newsreaders. We watched CBS because we trusted Walter Cronkite.

Several days a week, at the end of the newscast, Walter turned the desk over to Eric Sevareid for two minutes of analysis and commentary. We knew this wasn't news reporting because the word "Commentary" appeared at the bottom of the screen. Mr. Sevareid was voicing his opinions, and they were clearly labeled as such. You could never question what his colleague Walter Cronkite said because it was hard news, but you were free to agree or disagree with Mr. Sevareid's opinions.

Fast-forward half a century and take a look at today's media landscape, where there are more opinions than facts being broadcast, whether on cable TV news networks or on talk radio. Much of the programming on MSNBC and Fox News is pure opinion, dominated by a coterie of talking heads and their slates of like-minded guests, and CNN isn't much better. Turn on the radio and all you hear are the Hannitys, Limbaughs, and Becks and the occasional left-wing variation. It's all talk, all the time, with very little news to break up the conversation.

There's nothing wrong with espousing one's opinion—over the airwaves or online—as long as it's clearly understood as such. The problem comes when viewers, listeners, or readers take these opinions as facts and view the commentators as reporters. They're not. Sean Hannity and Rachel Maddow, as much as you might like or dislike them, are not journalists. They're commentators, offering their own opinions on the day's events. What they say may be interesting—and it might even be true—but it's always served up with that person's own particular brand of biases. It's not news, it's opinion—even if it's not always identified as such.

So when you see someone quoting their favorite left- or right-wing commentator, know that you're hearing that person's opinion. The facts of the matter may be different.

Satire

Don't confuse fake news stories and websites with satirical articles and sites. There are quite a few websites out there that manufacture humorous stories in the name of entertainment, and it's easy to mistake some of these sites with honest-to-goodness news sites or their mirror-image fake news cousins.

Take, for example, The Onion (www.theonion.com). This site started out in 1988 as a satirical print newspaper, akin to *National Lampoon* and similar rags of the time, and it eventually made the transition to an online publication. It has an established reputation as a source of humorous made-up news stories, with headlines like "Winner Didn't Know It Was Pie-Eating Contest," "Drugs Win Drug War," "CIA Realizes It's Been Using Black Highlighters All These Years," and "People Far Away from You Not Actually Smaller."

Satirical news stories aren't really fake news, but they're certainly not real news, either. They're meant to be funny and not to be taken seriously. If you run into one of these articles in your Facebook News Feed and feel the urge to laugh, it's probably satire.

Some Fake News Is Real News

There's another use of the term "fake news" that is important to recognize. It's when a person in power, most often a politician, dismisses actual news that he dislikes or disagrees with as fake news. In other words, when this person is the subject of a negative news story, instead of debating the charges, he attacks the news source itself by calling the whole thing "fake news."

Of course, just because someone doesn't like a particular news story doesn't make that story "fake" or the facts incorrect. The reality is that most news items painted as "fake" by persons of power aren't fake at all. Even the most powerful people in the world can't make a genuine news story fake just by saying so—but they can smear that news source in the minds of their followers.

Attacking real news as "fake" is not only disingenuous, it's also dangerous. There are lots of facts that I don't happen to personally like, but I can't dispute them *because they are facts*. Facts are *not* opinions; they don't become less true just because you don't like what they mean.

This co-opting of the previously useful phrase "fake news" to attack legitimate news sources throws the whole discussion of fake news into dispute. When someone mentions "fake news" today, it's more likely to be in reference to a negative news story than to describe actual fictitious news.

So, be wary of those who too quickly dismiss inconvenient truths as "fake news." You can't make bad news go away by questioning its validity. Facts are facts, even (and especially) if you don't like them.

How Fake News Is Distributed on Facebook

As you browse your News Feed for new posts from your Facebook friends, you're likely to find a broad mix of information and opinion. No doubt some of your friends like to post provocative thoughts on the current state of the world; others like to link to stories that reinforce their political and other views.

When you see these posts from your friends, keep one thing in mind:

Just because someone posts something on Facebook doesn't mean it's true.

If you remember nothing else from this chapter, remember that statement. Although Facebook can be a great source of news and information, it can also be a breeding ground for misinformation, lies, and propaganda. What makes Facebook so easy to use also makes it easy to spread rumor, innuendo, and plain old lies.

During the 2016 election season, for example, one analysis studied 156 fake political stories that were shared on Facebook. These stories were shared more than 122 million times. Yes, that's right—122 *million* people saw these 156 stories. That's a lot of people who were exposed to a relative small number of fake stories.

Another study found that during the final weeks of the 2016 presidential election, more than a quarter of American adults visited a page on a pro-Trump or pro-Clinton fake news website. These visits were often prompted by viewing fake news posts and advertisements on Facebook.

How do the people who create these fake news stories get people to view them? There are a number of different ways.

Phony Facebook Accounts

Purveyors of fake news often spread their stories by creating dozens or hundreds of phony Facebook accounts. Then they post a given story to all these fake accounts.

In addition, the fake users friend other Facebook users, often targeting like-minded users by detailing the user's behavior on the Facebook site. The humans or bots behind these fake accounts then expose their newfound friends to their fake posts in their News Feeds. As friends of the fake friend view these stories in their News Feeds, the stories spread virally to thousands of other users.

Facebook Ads

The transmitters of fake news also purchase advertisements on the Facebook site to reach more viewers. These ads, targeted at specific types of users (by age, gender, location, and interests), can appear as traditional ads, in the sidebar beside the News Feed, or as "sponsored posts" within a person's News Feed itself. Both types of ads can easily be confused for organic content (posts generated by real users), which lends them more weight than they might otherwise have.

How widespread is this technique? As one example, Facebook has publicly admitted that Russian operatives placed more than 3,000 politically divisive ads during the 2016 election season. Who knows how many users saw these ads for fake content?

Sharing Fake Stories

Finally, users who see fake news stories in other media often copy and share links to these stories in their Facebook News Feeds, thinking that its real news. Fake news creators place their fake stories in lots of different media, online and off, thus increasing the odds of the stories being shared by readers in their Facebook feeds.

How widespread is this type of fake news sharing? A Pew Research Center survey revealed that almost a quarter (23%) of Americans said they have shared a fake news story, with 14% saying they shared a story they knew was fake at the time. That's a lot of people sharing stuff they later recognized was fake.

Why Some People Believe Fake News

On the surface, the claims that drive most fake news seem totally outrageous. Why, in the Pizzagate scenario, would a presidential candidate be involved with a human-trafficking operation—and from a small pizza joint, at that? Why would doctors knowingly squelch a miracle cure for cancer—and why would such a cure come from a common garden weed?

None of it really makes any sense, yet millions of people continue to believe the fake news they find online. Why?

Confirmation Bias

One reason some people believe fake news is because they want to believe it. If you're predisposed to a particular position or belief, when you hear a "fact" that reinforces your belief, you tend to believe it. If, on the other hand, you hear something that runs counter to what you believe, you tend to discount it. That's just human nature.

We all suffer, to one degree or another, from something the experts call *confirmation bias*. This is the tendency to interpret new information as confirmation of our existing beliefs. When someone introduces a new fact, we twist it around so that it seems to support our prior opinions. And if we can't, then we discount that new fact as being somehow fake or illegitimate.

In a 2015 article in *Psychology Today*, Dr. Shahram Heshmat described confirmation bias as "once we have formed a view, we embrace information that confirms that view while ignoring, or rejecting, information that casts doubt on it… We pick out those bits of data that make us feel good because they confirm our prejudices. Thus, we may become prisoners of our assumptions."

Confirmation bias explains why we're susceptible to certain fake news stories. If a given story supports our views on a given topic, we're likely to believe it. On the other hand, if a real news story contradicts our views on that topic, we're likely to view that legitimate story as "fake."

Intuition Over Fact

Some people rely heavily on facts. They don't like or trust hearsay and rumors. They need to see the facts that back up any statement. They tend not to believe fake news.

Other people are more likely to trust their intuition. They don't need, want, or look for a lot of facts to trust statements that strike them as believable. These people are more susceptible to the allure of fake news.

A 2017 Ohio State University/University of Michigan study asked participants about several controversial issues: climate change, well-known conspiracy theories, and the unconfirmed link between vaccines and autism. The study revealed that people who agreed with the statement "I trust my gut to tell me what's true and what's not" were more likely to believe fake news and conspiracy theories about these topics. Those who agreed with the statement "Evidence is more important than whether something feels true" were shown to be less likely to believe such falsehoods.

Hope

When it comes to some types of non-politcal fake news, people want to believe that there is hope. If you are the victim of a serious disease, you want to fervently believe that somewhere out there exists a pill, a treatment, an elixir you can take that will cure you. If you're deep in debt or can't find a job, you want to believe that the latest work-from-home scheme really does pay $40 per hour.

When things are tough, we need to believe that there's some sort of hope out there. When conventional means offer little hope, we reach beyond. It's the same desperation that has fueled miracle cures and get-rich-quick schemes for generations.

Echo Chamber Effect

When you combine fake news with the speed and efficiency of the Internet and social media, you amplify the problem. You see, one of the bad things about Facebook and other social media, and the Internet in general, is that you can filter it so that you only see those posts and stories that you want to see. You only have to visit those websites you want; you don't have to view any sites you don't like. The same thing with your Facebook News Feed; you see the opinions of your friends and the people you follow, and don't see any the opinions of anyone else.

This also means that you tend to see the same stories and information multiple times. You might read the initial source of the information and then see that story reposted by one or more of your friends. The more often you see something, the more likely you are to view it as a fact—even if it isn't.

Social scientists call this the *illusory truth effect*. Put simply, people tend to view statements they've seen before as true—whether they are or not. As psychologist Lisa Fazio of Vanderbilt University in Tennessee put it in a 2017 interview with *Vox*, the more you hear something, the more "you'll have this gut-level feeling that maybe it's true."

This creates a kind of *echo chamber*, where you only hear from people and sources like you and never get exposed to any opposing views. The echo chamber reinforces your existing views and never challenges them. You keep hearing more and more of the same thing and less and less of anything remotely different—which makes you even more susceptible to fake news that buttresses what you already believe.

How to Tell Real News from Fake News

With all the fake news and outright lies circulating on Facebook, how do you distinguish the false facts from the real ones? After all, if you can't trust everything you see online (and you can't), then you have to do your homework to separate fact from fiction. No one else will do it for you.

See If Facebook Flags It

Facebook is far and away the most used social medium today. Unfortunately, Facebook has also been the most common vehicle for fake news and misleading information due to users sharing inaccurate posts with their friends on the site.

As such, you need to be especially wary of the "news stories" and web links shared by your friends on Facebook. There's a halfway decent chance that any given news item you see shared in your Facebook News Feed is biased or fraudulent.

Facebook realizes this and is trying various approaches to identify or remove obvious fake posts and propaganda. Initially, Facebook tried to "flag" fake news stories on its site but found that putting a red flag on a story actually encouraged people to read it. (That's called an *unintended consequence*.)

Instead, Facebook now includes a Show More Information About This Article (sometimes an "i" icon) link on questionable posts. Click or tap the link/icon and you see more information about the news source; the hope is that users will click the links to read more reliable reporting on controversial topics.

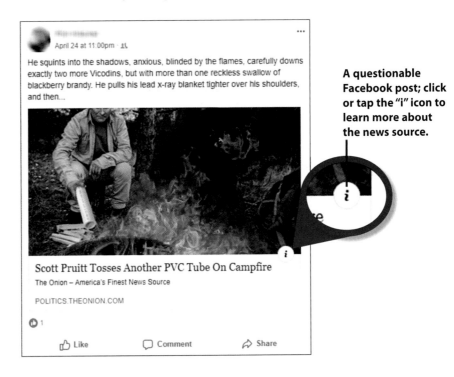

A questionable Facebook post; click or tap the "i" icon to learn more about the news source.

In addition, if Facebook's in-house fact-checkers classify a story as fake, it is demoted in users' News Feeds. This makes the fake story harder for users to find, thus mitigating its impact and spread.

Facebook has also introduced a way for you to report posts that you think contain false information. Tap or click the More (three dots) button in the top-right corner of a post, tap or click Report Post, and then, on the Help Us Understand What's Happening screen or panel, select It's a False News Story. You can then opt to mark this post as false news; block all future posts from this person; hide all posts from this person; or message this individual to let him know you think this article is false.

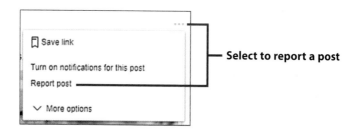

Select to report a post

Consider the Source

When you see a questionable post in your News Feed, you should consider where that piece of information came from. Some sources are more reliable than others—and some are obviously fake.

For example, if you see an article shared from CNN or *The New York Times* or the AP, it's real news. If the article comes from a source that's less well known, not known to you at all, or known to be a fake news site, you should treat that article with a grain of salt.

It's Not All Good

Check the URL

Be especially wary of fake news sites designed to look like legitimate news sites. You can often tell by a slight difference in their web URLs. For example, there's the legitimate CBS News site at www.cbsnews.com, and the fake site at www.cbsnews.com.co. That little extra ".co" at the end is a completely different web address that leads to a completely different—and completely fake—site.

Verify with Multiple Sources

If you're not sure about a given news article—either the article itself or the article's source—then see if you can find a similar story from another source. That means opening up your web browser and doing an Internet search, or (if you're on Facebook) just searching from with the Search box at the top of the News Feed.

If you can't find any corroborating stories, then it's likely the original story was fake. If you do find similar stories, but they're all from similarly questionable sources, then the original story might still be fake. If, on the other hand, you find similar stories from trusted sources, then the story is probably okay.

Consider What Is Being Said

Sometimes the best way to tell whether a story is fake is to simply trust your nose. If it smells fake, it probably is.

For example, would you believe a story with the headline "Bombshell Science Study Reveals Internal Heat from Earth's Hot Core Is What's Causing Greenland's Ice Sheets to Slide"? Although this sounds interesting, it just doesn't seem likely. It smells funny, and it is funny, too.

This doesn't always go the other direction, however. Some fake news is designed to sound legitimate, even if it isn't. A headline like "Firefighter Jailed 30 Days by Atheist Mayor for Praying at Scene of Fire" isn't wildly outlandish, and it might even sound like something that could happen. It might pass your smell test, even though it's fake from start to finish.

All in all, though, trust your instincts. If something doesn't seem plausible, dig into it a little more to evaluate the source and legitimacy of the article. Don't accept questionable content at face value.

Check with the Fact Checkers

When I'm not sure whether something is fake or real, I consult a site that specializes in debunking fake news and other dubious stories. There are several good fact-checking sites online, including the following:

- **Media Bias/Fact Check (www.mediabiasfactcheck.com).** How do you know if a news source is trustworthy, biased, or just plain lying to you? The Media Bias/

Fact Check site lists most known major media outlets, online and off, and ranks them according to perceived bias. Enter the name of a particular news website or organization to see whether they have a leftward bias or a right-leaning bias, or if they're relatively unbiased. The more centered a site's bias—and the lower the conspiracy level—the more likely the stories it posts are truthful.

- **PolitiFact (www.politifact.com).** This is a good site to help determine the truthfulness of politically related news items. PolitiFact relies on a team of staffers to research and determine the accuracy of statements made by elected officials, politicians, and pundits. Accuracy is rated on the site's Truth-O-Meter, in degrees from True to False.

- **Snopes (www.snopes.com).** This is a reliable source for debunking falsehoods or confirming truthful information you find on the Internet. Its original and primary focus is on debunking urban legends, but it's become a fact-checking site for all sorts of fake (and real) news articles. Just enter the title of the questionable article and Snopes tells you if it's true, false, or somewhere in between.

If a Politician Says It's Fake, It's Probably Real

Finally, remember that many politicians—including the president himself—like to label negative news stories they don't like as "fake news," even though they aren't. So if a president or senator or congressperson (or one of their spokespeople) labels a story as fake news, it's probably real news. Don't fall for their misdirection!

How *Not* to Spread Fake News

Hopefully the information in this chapter has alerted you to the problem of fake news and fraudulent information you might find on Facebook. You've learned what fake news is and how to identify it.

Your challenge from here is to not only avoid being influenced by fake news, but also to not spread it to your friends and family. To be a responsible social media user, you need to keep your News Feed as factual as possible and avoid spreading information of questionable validity.

Here's what you need to do.

Read It Before You Share It

Believe it or not, more than half the people who share stories via Facebook don't actually read the stories they share. A lot of folks read only the headline and post it without reading anything. That's irresponsible.

If you're going to share something with people you know and respect, respect them enough to read the thing you're sharing. You might discover, on closer inspection, that the article is obviously fraudulent, that it doesn't actually say what the headline promises, or that you disagree with what it ends up saying. If you want your friends to read it, the least you can do is read it first.

Check It Out Before You Share It

Don't share things that you suspect are fake. Use all the techniques you've learned in this chapter, including the Snopes and Media Bias/Fact Check websites, to check the validity of the article; don't just blindly repost things you see in your News Feed. Make sure it's factual before you share it.

If Someone Questions It, Remove It

If you somehow end up posting something that isn't factual, and someone points out to you that that's the case, go back and delete. Facebook lets you delete a post after you've posted; you should do this if you discover you've posted some fake news. It's a good way to correct your mistakes. (You may even want to create a new post revealing the new information you have about the first post, to completely clear the air.)

Bottom line, you need to be careful about what you share on social media. There's a lot of phony stuff out there, and you don't want to be duped into sharing it with people who trust you. Keep their trust by not posting fake news.

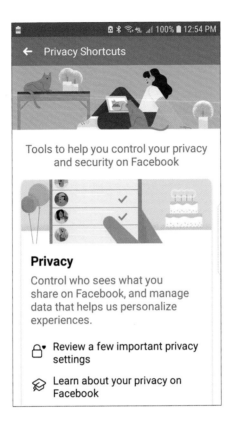

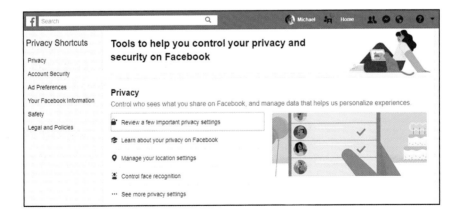

In this chapter, you find out how to keep your private information from becoming public on the Facebook site.

Managing Your Privacy on Facebook

Facebook is a social network, and being social means sharing one's personal information with others. In Facebook's case, it's likely that you're sharing a lot of your private information not just with your friends but also with Facebook and its partners and advertisers.

And it's not just your contact information. Facebook is also tracking everything you do on its site—the pages you visit, the groups you join, and the posts you like. Facebook also tracks the people you friend and the people they friend. It's a lot of information.

Fortunately, it's possible to keep most of your personal information personal when you're using Facebook— but it requires some work on your part.

What Facebook Tracks—and Why

All the information that you share and that Facebook collects poses a problem if you'd rather keep some things private. If you share everything with everyone, all sorts of information can get out—and be seen by people you don't want to see it. The problem is only exacerbated if Facebook shares the information it collects, too.

Facebook has the ability to track not only the personal and contact information you enter on your profile page, but also every single thing you do on the Facebook site, which includes

- Status updates you post

- Other posts you like

- Posts you share

- Comments you make on posts

- The amount of time you spend looking at or reading specific posts

- Your friends (and the amount of time you spend visiting friends' profile pages)

- Any payments you make to purchase apps, products, or services on the Facebook site

- Devices you use to access Facebook—computers, phones, tablets, and so on.

Note that Facebook also collects this information from other users who might be reading your posts or interacting with you. Thus, Facebook uses your friends' activities to learn more about you, too.

In addition, Facebook tracks your activity on sites on which you've signed in with your Facebook account. Facebook not only tracks the individual sites you sign into, but also what you do when you're on those sites.

Why does Facebook track all this activity? For a number of reasons.

First, Facebook tracks your activity to decide what posts you see in your News Feed. That's the Top Content model, where your prior interactions determine the future content of your Feed. If you spend more time interacting with posts from a given friend or group, you'll see more posts for that person or group in the future.

Second, Facebook uses the information it gathers to better target the ads you see on its site. This is why you might see an ad for running shoes after you make a post about jogging in your neighborhood. It seems eerily prescient and intrusive, but otherwise you'd see a bunch of random ads instead. (And you'll always see ads, no matter what; that's how Facebook makes money.)

Note that Facebook doesn't sell your personal data to third parties. (That's a good thing.) However, any site you've logged into with your Facebook credentials can access and share your personal data, as can any app or game you use on the Facebook site. (You give them your permission to do so when you agree to use the app—which you probably didn't catch before you clicked.)

Configuring Privacy Options

Facebook lets you configure a variety of options that affect your privacy on its site. You can control who sees the posts you make and the photos you upload, as well as manage the data that Facebook collects about you.

The majority of these privacy options are centralized on the Privacy Shortcuts page. You can configure these options from either the Facebook mobile app or, on your computer, the Facebook website.

Review Important Privacy Settings

You control your main privacy settings by conducting what Facebook calls a Privacy Checkup.

(1) On the Facebook website, click the Quick Help icon on the toolbar and then click Privacy Checkup and proceed to step 3. *Or…*

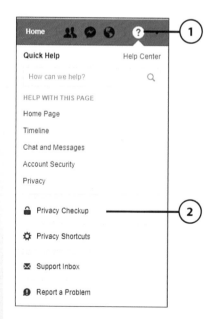

② In the Facebook mobile app, tap the More icon, tap to expand the Settings & Privacy section, and then tap Privacy Shortcuts.

③ The Privacy Shortcuts screen opens. Tap or click Review a Few Important Privacy Settings.

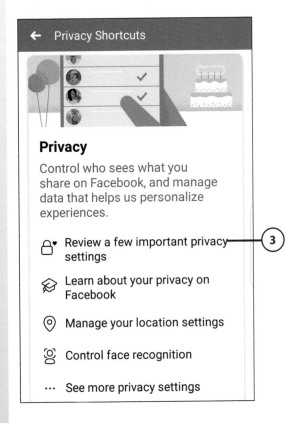

(4) In the mobile app, you're prompted to start your Privacy Checkup. Tap Next.

(5) Tap or click the Privacy button to select who can see your next post.

(6) Select Public to let everyone on Facebook see the post.

(7) Select Friends to make a post visible only to people on your friends list.

(8) Select Friends Except and then select specific people or groups who you don't want to see the post.

(9) Tap See More on your mobile device to view more privacy options. (If necessary on the website, click More.)

CLOSE   NEXT ◄─── (4)

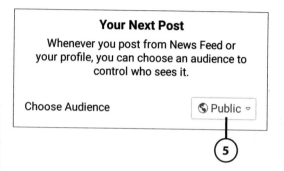

Your Next Post

Whenever you post from News Feed or your profile, you can choose an audience to control who sees it.

Choose Audience   🌐 Public ▽

|
(5)

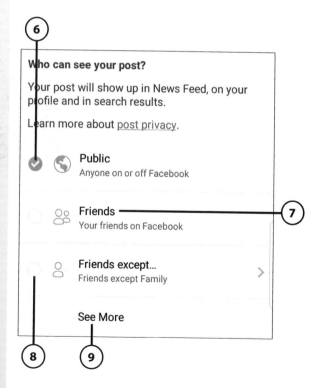

(6)

Who can see your post?

Your post will show up in News Feed, on your profile and in search results.

Learn more about <u>post privacy</u>.

✓ 🌐 **Public**
       Anyone on or off Facebook

   👥 **Friends** ─────────────── (7)
       Your friends on Facebook

   👤 **Friends except...**   ›
       Friends except Family

       See More

(8)   (9)

(10) Select Specific Friends to show this post only to those friends you select.

(11) Select Only Me to hide this post from everyone except yourself.

(12) Select See All to share this post with a specific list of individuals.

(13) In the mobile app, tap Done to return to the Your Next Post screen.

(14) Tap or click Next.

(15) The Your Profile Privacy screen opens. Tap or click the Privacy button next to each contact item to select who can see it—Public, Friends, Only Me, and so on. Select Only Me to hide this information from everyone else on Facebook.

(16) Tap or click Next.

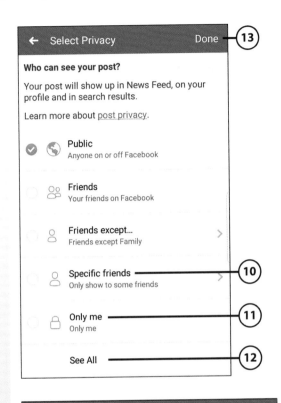

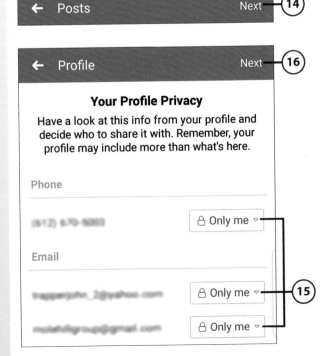

17 The Your App Privacy screen opens. All the apps and websites you interact with are listed here. To remove any app or website, tap or click to select it then tap or click the Remove button.

18 Tap or click the Privacy button for any app or website to change who can see that item—Public, Friends, and so on. Tap or click Only Me to hide this item from everyone on Facebook.

19 Tap or click Next.

20 Your Privacy Checkup is complete. Tap or click the Close button.

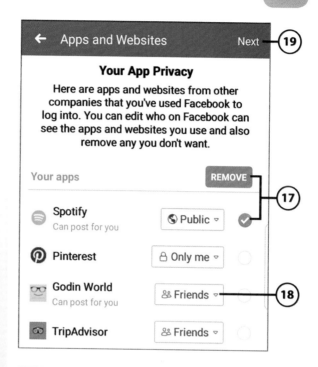

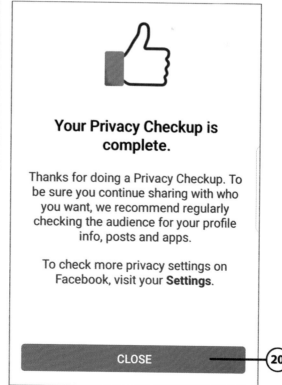

Manage Your Location Settings

If you're using the Facebook app on a mobile device, you can configure various settings related to how Facebook uses your current location. (These settings aren't available if you're using the Facebook website on your computer.)

1. From the Privacy Shortcuts screen, go to the Privacy section and tap Manage Your Location Settings.

2. Tap Find Wi-Fi to receive a daily notification from a nearby public Wi-Fi hotspot when you're away from home.

3. Tap Nearby Friends to let people you choose see you when you're connected to a nearby Wi-Fi network or hotspot.

4. Tap Weather to receive daily weather updates in your News Feed. (Not available on iOS version.)

5. Tap Place Tips to receive information in your News Feed about nearby places. (Not available on iOS version.)

6. Tap "on" Location History to keep a history of where you've logged onto Facebook on your mobile devices.

7. Tap View Your Location History to view where you've recently logged onto Facebook.

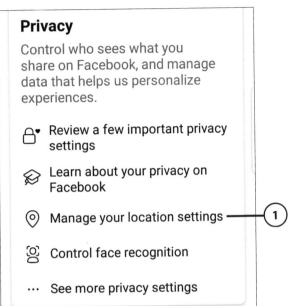

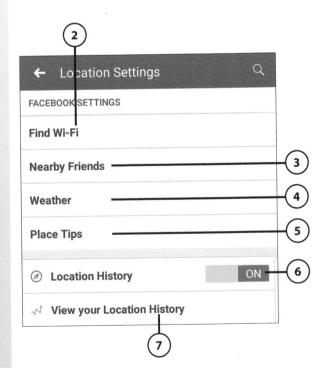

Control Facebook's Face Recognition

Facebook likes to connect people with each other. This is often done via "tagging," where one user can tag ("who are you with?") another user in a status update or photo without asking the other person. When you're tagged, you're connected to that post or photo, whether you want to be or not—which can be an invasion of your privacy.

One of the ways that Facebook encourages tagging is by suggesting people to tag when someone posts a photo. Facebook does this via facial recognition technology; it compares a given photo with the millions of other photos uploaded to its site and tries to match a new face with one it already knows.

So if someone uploads a picture of someone who looks like you, Facebook suggests that you be tagged in that photo. That's fine, unless that's not really you— or if the photo is one you'd rather not be associated with. Fortunately, you can turn off these photo tag suggestions.

It's Not All Good

You Can Still Be Tagged

Just because you turn off Facebook's ability to suggest your name when someone uploads a photo, that doesn't mean you can't be tagged in that photo. The person who uploaded the photo can still manually tag you, even if your name isn't automatically suggested.

(1) From the Privacy Shortcuts screen either in the mobile app or on the Facebook website, tap or click Control Face Recognition.

Privacy

Control who sees what you share on Facebook, and manage data that helps us personalize experiences.

⌂• Review a few important privacy settings

◈ Learn about your privacy on Facebook

◉ Manage your location settings

⚏ Control face recognition ———— (1)

(**2**) Facial recognition is enabled by default. To turn it off, click or tap Do You Want Facebook to Be Able to Recognize You in Photos and Videos? and then select No.

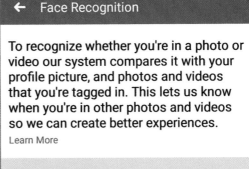

Configuring Account Security Options

Facebook lets you control which personal information is stored on its site and who can see that information.

Review Account Security Settings

Your account security settings are accessible from the Privacy Shortcuts screen both in the mobile app and on the Facebook website.

(**1**) From the Privacy Shortcuts screen, scroll to the Account Security section.

(**2**) Tap or click Update Your Personal Information to edit your name, email address, phone number, and Legacy Contact settings.

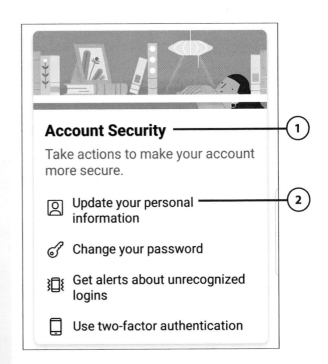

3 Tap or click Change Your Password to change your Facebook password.

4 Tap Get Alerts About Unrecognized Logins to receive a notification when you or someone else tries to log in to your Facebook account from an unfamiliar location or web browser.

5 Tap Use Two-Factor Authentication to require an extra login code when you log in to your Facebook account from an unrecognized phone or computer.

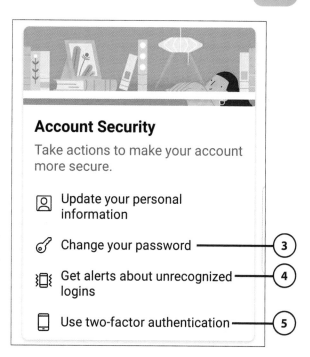

Configuring Advertising Preferences

Facebook can share the data it collects with a variety of third parties, including advertisers, apps, and websites. This access used to be kept somewhat secretive, but Facebook is now more open about what it shares with whom. You can even tell Facebook *not* to share selected data, in many cases.

Review Facebook Ad Settings

Facebook collects and analyzes a variety of data that it uses to select which ads from which advertisers you see on its site. If Facebook, for example, thinks that you're married, with a college education, and like *Star Trek* and HGTV, it shows you ads for products and services that relate to these interests.

You can, however, view what Facebook feeds to its advertisers—and, to a degree, edit this information. You do this from the Privacy Shortcuts screen, from either the mobile app or Facebook website.

1. From the Privacy Shortcuts screen, scroll to the Ad Preferences section.

2. Tap or click Review Your Ad Preferences.

3. In the Your Interests section, select a topic to view and edit all the interests you've professed in that area.

4. Tap or click Advertisers You've Interacted With to view entities who have served ads to you or remove ads from a given advertiser.

5. Tap or click Your Information to view specific information Facebook knows about you.

6. Tap or click Ad Settings to view and edit the types of ads that Facebook serves to your News Feed.

7. Tap or click Hide Ad Topics to turn off specific types of ads.

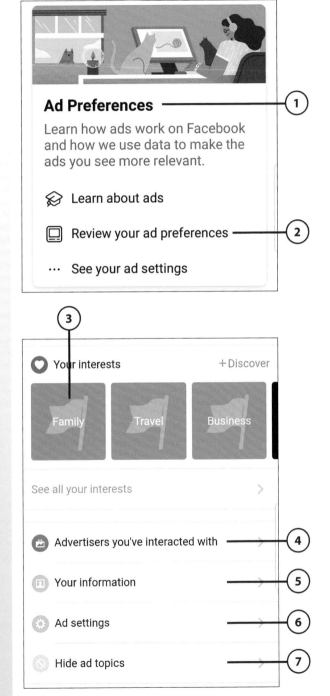

Viewing Your Facebook Information

Facebook collects a lot of data about you but lets you see what it's collected. (You'll be surprised how much it collects!)

Access and Manage Your Information

You can view and manage the data Facebook collects about you from the Privacy Shortcuts screen, from either the mobile app or the Facebook website.

(1) From the Privacy Shortcuts screen, scroll to the Your Facebook Information section.

(2) Tap or click Access Your Information to view your posts, photos and videos, comments, likes and reactions, friends, people you're following and those who are following you, messages, groups, events, profile information, pages, Marketplace activity, payment history, saved items, places you've created, apps and websites you log into using Facebook, ad-related info, information associated with your Facebook account, search history, location history, calls and messages, and security and login information.

(3) Tap or click See Your Activity Log to view a log of your recent Facebook activity.

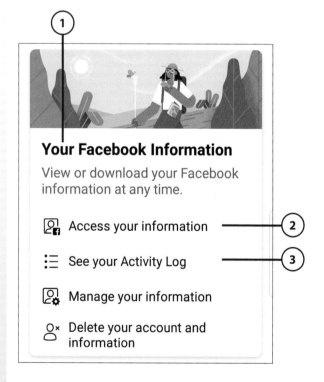

Your Facebook Information

View or download your Facebook information at any time.

- Access your information
- See your Activity Log
- Manage your information
- Delete your account and information

(4) Tap or click Manage Your Information to edit your personal information.

(5) Tap or click Delete Your Account and Information to delete your Facebook account.

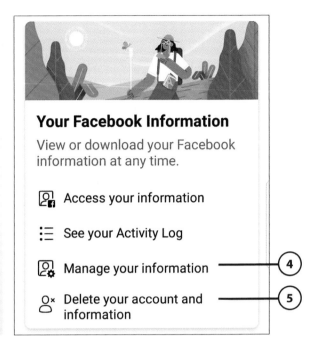

Your Facebook Information

View or download your Facebook information at any time.

Access your information

See your Activity Log

Manage your information ——— (4)

Delete your account and ——— (5)
information

>>>Go Further
FACEBOOK'S PRIVACY PROBLEMS

Facebook has a problem with privacy. Over the years, it has let numerous third parties have access to user information, including just about everything you and your friends have done on the Facebook site—and you haven't known it was happening.

Perhaps the biggest breach of privacy was unearthed in the aftermath of the 2016 presidential elections. A company named Cambridge Analytica gathered information on up to 87 million Facebook users and used that data to identify voter personalities and attempt to influence their vote (in favor of the Donald Trump campaign, its client).

How it worked was simple. Back in 2014, Cambridge Analytica created one of those cute little personality quizzes, called *thisisyourdigitallife*, in which users answer a series of seemingly innocuous questions and then the app says what kind of personality they are. In the process of taking this quiz, users gave the app permission to access their Facebook data—and the data of everyone on their friends list. More than 270,000 users took the quiz, which ultimately harvested personal data on close to 87 million users. (Everybody who took the quiz had a few hundred friends, it seems.) Whereas the people who took the quiz gave (tacit) permission to use their data, the other 87 million or so users gave no such permission.

The problem was, back in 2014, Facebook's privacy rules permitted third parties to access the data of participant's friends without their permission. A year or so later, Facebook changed its rules to prohibit this scraping of data. So a company trying to do this in 2016 would only have garnered the data from the people who took the quiz, not their friends. But back in 2014, when Cambridge Analytica offered the "quiz," this sort of behavior was allowed.

Not surprisingly, when the Cambridge Analytica situation came to light, it garnered a fair amount of negative publicity. Mark Zuckerberg, the founder and CEO of Facebook, had to appear before both Senate and Congressional committees to answer questions relating to this issue. It was a big deal.

The specific issue—sharing data without users' awareness or permission—had already been addressed with updated Facebook privacy guidelines. The ongoing issue, however, that Facebook uses your information and behavior to not only offer up a better user experience but also to make money (by selling ads based on your activity), remains.

To get the most out of Facebook, you need to let the company know as much about you and what you do on its site (and beyond) as you're comfortable with. If you don't let Facebook know all this about you, not only will you have a less fulfilling experience, Facebook also won't make as much money from targeted advertising. And if Facebook doesn't make as much money from advertisers, it might have to start charging users.

You see, the bigger issue here, well beyond Facebook, is that we all like to get stuff for free. We want free social networking from Facebook, free search from Google, free information from Wikipedia, and so on. However, those services you get for free have to be paid for: There are programmers to be paid, office space to be leased, equipment to be purchased, and so forth. Typically, the companies that offer the services pay for the costs through advertising. Advertisers pay good money to get in front of potential customers, and the more targeted their ads, the more they're willing to pay.

So if you want Facebook to remain free, you have to accept those annoying ads that keep cropping up in your News Feed. And you have to accept that Facebook will use the information it collects about you to help sell those ads. In a way, Facebook isn't the product here—you are.

Unless you want to start paying to use Facebook and Twitter and Google and all the other good stuff on the Internet, you have to accept both advertising and some invasion of your privacy. The only alternatives are for Facebook et al. to start charging for their services or for you to stop using those services. In fact, the only way to ensure complete privacy and security is to not use any online services at all.

Not surprisingly, some people are choosing this latter option. Post-Cambridge Analytica scandal, a fair number of Facebook users have stopped using the service and deleted their accounts. Not a lot, but some. That might be the best route for some people, although it does take you out of the social-media loop. (Other social media, such as Twitter, have the identical problem, of course.)

If this works for you, great. Otherwise, follow the instructions in this chapter to minimize your privacy risk and still get the most you can out of Facebook and other social media. There may be no perfect solution to this issue, but you can do what you can do.

In this chapter, you find out how to view photos and videos that your friends have shared on Facebook, as well as how to upload your own photos and videos for your friends to see.

10

Viewing and Sharing Photos and Videos

Sharing pictures and home movies is a great way to show your friends and family what you've been up to. Everybody loves looking at pictures, still or moving—whether they're vacation photos or home movies of your cute kids or grandkids.

It should come as no surprise that Facebook is the largest photo-sharing site on the Internet. (It's pretty big for sharing videos, too.) It's easy to upload photos or videos to a Facebook photo album and then share them with all your Facebook friends. It's equally easy to view your friends' photos and videos on Facebook—and download and print those photos you'd like to keep for posterity.

Viewing Friends' Photos and Videos

Some people on Facebook post photos and videos as part of their regular status updates. These items appear in your News Feed, as part of the stream of your friends' status updates.

Other Facebook users upload their photos to special photo albums they've created in their Facebook accounts. This is a more serious and organized way to share a large number of photos online. You can view these photo albums from the user's profile page.

View Photos in Your News Feed

When a friend posts a photo as part of a status update, that photo appears in your News Feed. You can view photos at that small size within the News Feed, or you can enlarge them to view them full screen.

(1) Within your News Feed, all photos appear within the bodies of the accompanying status updates. Some status updates may have multiple pictures attached. To view a larger version of any picture, click or tap the photo in the post.

(2) If you're using the Facebook website, this displays the photo within its own *lightbox*—a special window superimposed over the News Feed. To view the photo even larger, click the Enter Fullscreen icon at the top-right corner of the photo. (To exit fullscreen mode, press Esc on your computer keyboard or the X at the top-right corner of the screen.)

3 If you're using the Facebook mobile app, you see the photo on its own photo page. Tap your phone's Back button to return to your News Feed.

View a Video in Your News Feed

Any videos that your friends upload to Facebook also show up in your News Feed. You'll see a video as a thumbnail image that may or may not have a play-back arrow on top; playing the video is as easy as clicking that image.

YouTube Videos

Users can also share videos they find on YouTube, Vimeo, and other video-sharing sites. These videos also appear in your friends' News Feeds. To view the video on the YouTube or Vimeo site, click or tap the video's title to open that site in a new tab in your web browser or in the appropriate app on your mobile device. (Click or tap the video itself, and it plays in the News Feed.)

(1) Navigate to the status update that contains the video, and click or tap the video thumbnail to play the video. In some cases, video playback begins in the News Feed itself. In other cases, playback begins on a separate video page. (The video may play automatically when you scroll to the post, but without sound—kind of like a muted preview. If this is the case, you need to click or tap the video to play it back with sound.)

(2) To view the video at a larger size on the Facebook website, mouse over the video to display the playback controls at the bottom and click the Full Screen icon. Press Esc on your computer keyboard to return to normal playback mode.

(3) To pause the playback on the Facebook website, mouse over the video to display the playback controls, and then click the Pause button—which now changes to a Play button. To pause the playback in the mobile app, tap the screen to display the Pause button, and then tap it. Click or tap the Play button or tap the screen again to resume playback.

(4) Click and drag the volume control to raise or lower the playback volume on the Facebook website. (If you're using the mobile app, use your phone's up and down volume buttons to raise or lower the playback volume.)

(5) Click and drag (or tap and drag) the time slider to move to another point in the video.

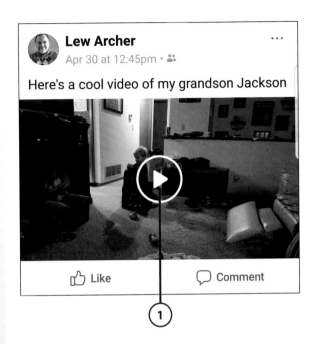

Auto Playback

To turn auto playback on or off on the Facebook website, go to the Settings page, select the Videos tab on the left, and then click the button next to the Auto-Play Videos option. Select On to always play videos or Off to never engage Auto-Play.

View a Friend's Photo Albums

More serious photographers—and people with a lot of photos to share— organize their Facebook photos into individual photo albums. These are virtual versions of those traditional photo albums you've kept in the past. You can then navigate through a friend's photo albums to find and view the photos you like.

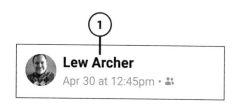

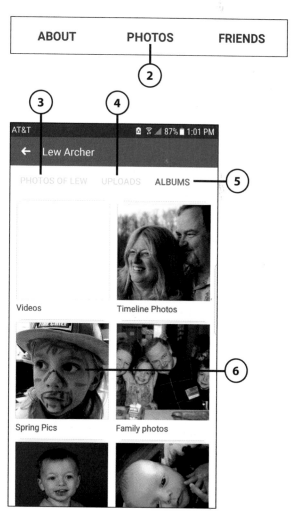

(1) Click or tap your friend's name or profile picture anywhere on Facebook to open his profile page.

(2) Click or tap Photos to display your friend's Photos page.

(3) Click or tap Photos of *Friend* to view all photos of your friend.

(4) Tap Uploads (or, on the website, click *Friend's* Photos) to view all photos posted by your friend.

(5) Click or tap Albums to view photos as posted in their photo albums.

(6) Click or tap to open the selected album, and then click or tap any photo to view it in the photo viewer.

View All of a Friend's Videos

All the videos a friend has uploaded are displayed in a Videos album on the Albums tab of the friend's Photos page. You can play back any video from here.

(1) Go to your friend's Photos page and click or tap Albums to display your friend's photo albums.

(2) Click or tap the Videos album to display all this person's videos.

Upload Order

The videos in the Videos album are organized by date uploaded. Newest uploads are displayed first.

(3) Click or tap a video thumbnail to play that video.

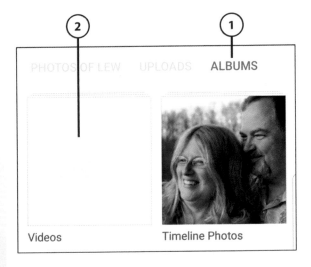

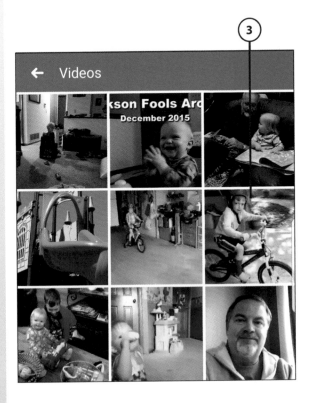

>>>*Go Further*

LIKING, COMMENTING ON, AND SHARING PHOTOS AND VIDEOS

You can like, comment on, and even share your friends' photos and videos. There are a number of ways to do these things.

If the photo or video appears in your News Feed, you can comment, like, or share it just as you would a normal status update. (Not all items can be shared; this depends on your friend's privacy settings for that item.) Just click or tap the appropriate link and proceed as normal.

You can also perform any of these actions from the photo or video viewer page. Again, click or tap Like, Comment, or Share to do what you want to do.

Tag Yourself in a Friend's Photo

If you find yourself in a photo that a friend has taken and uploaded to Facebook, you can "tag" yourself in that photo. When you're tagged in a photo, that photo appears in your Facebook timeline, in your friends' News Feeds, and on your Facebook photo albums page, on the Photos of You tab. This is easiest to do on the Facebook website, using your web browser.

(1) Display the photo in the photo viewer, mouse over the photo to display the menu at the bottom of the photo, and then click Tag Photo.

(2) Mouse over your face in the photo. A box appears around your face, with a text box underneath.

(3) Click within the text box to display a list of suggested names. Click your name in the list (it's probably the first one listed), or enter your name into the text box.

(4) Your name is now tagged to your face in this photo. Click Done Tagging to finish.

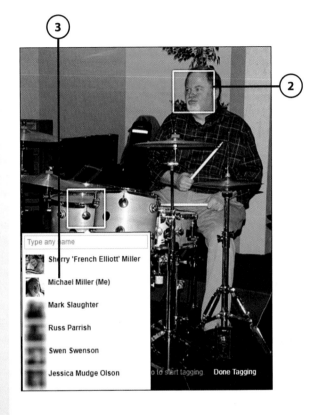

It's Not All Good

Removing Your Name from a Photo—Or Removing a Photo

You might not want to be tagged in a given picture. Perhaps the photo shows you doing something you shouldn't be doing. Maybe the photo is just a bad picture you don't particularly like. Or maybe you just don't like your name or face being out there on the Internet without your permission. In any instance, Facebook enables you to remove your name from any photo tagged by a friend; you can even request that a given photo be completely removed from the Facebook site.

To do this, display the photo and mouse over the photo to display the menu at the bottom of the photo. Click Options and then click Remove Tag; this displays the Remove Tag panel.

To remove your tag from the photo, click Okay.

Download a Photo

If you find a friend's photo that you really like, you can download it to your own computer, for your own personal use.

1. On your computer, display the photo in the photo viewer and mouse over the photo to display the menu at the bottom of the photo. Then click Options.

2. Click Download. On some systems the photo is automatically downloaded; on others, you need to click Save to use the Save As dialog box to save the photo.

3. On your phone, tap to open the photo; then tap the More (three-dot) icon.

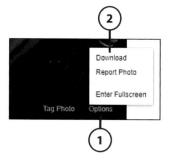

(4) Tap Save to Phone, and the photo
is automatically downloaded to
your device.

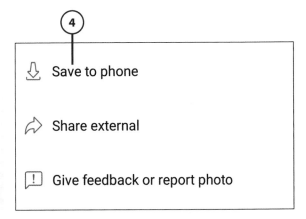

Sharing Your Photos and Videos with Friends

Whether you take pictures and videos with your smartphone, tablet, or digital
camera, you can share them all on Facebook with your friends and family. You
can share directly from your mobile device or from your computer—after you've
transferred your photos to your PC, of course.

Share a Photo or Video in a Status Update on the Facebook Website

Facebook lets you share any photo
or video as a status update, which
means all your friends should see them
in their News Feeds. Your uploaded
photos and videos also end up on your
Photos page, accessible from your profile page for all your friends to view.

We'll look first at how to upload photos and videos from your computer,
using the Facebook website.

(1) From the News Feed page, go
to the Publisher box and click
Photo/Video to display the Open
dialog box.

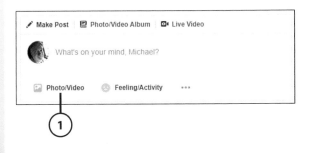

2 Navigate to and select the photo or video file(s) you want to upload. You can upload a single video file or multiple photo files. (To select more than one file on your computer, hold down the Ctrl key while you click each filename.)

3 Click Open.

4 You're returned to the Publisher box or screen with your photo(s) added. Click to add another picture, if you want.

5 If you like, enter a short text message describing the photo(s) or video.

6 Check to post to your News Feed or Your Story (or both).

7 Click Post.

Processing Videos

When you upload a video, Facebook must process it into the proper format to distribute on its site. This might take several minutes. You should be informed when the processing is complete; you can then edit the video description if you like, or select a thumbnail image for longer videos.

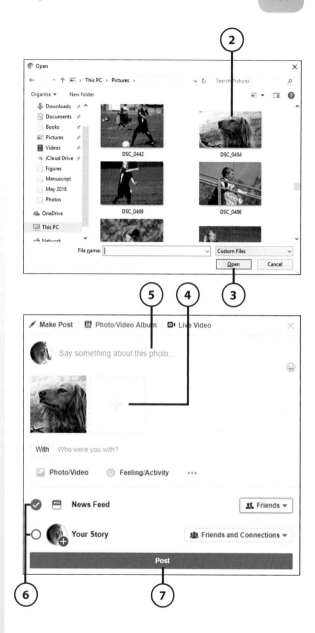

Share a Photo or Video from Your Mobile Phone

If you use your mobile phone to take photos, it's even easier to post those photos to Facebook. You don't have to transfer your phone photos to your computer first (although you can); Facebook lets you upload photos directly from your phone, using Facebook's mobile app. (This example uses Facebook's Android app; the iOS app works similarly.)

1. Use your phone's camera to take a picture, and then tap to open that picture in your phone's photo or gallery app.

2. Tap Share.

3. From the available options, tap Facebook.

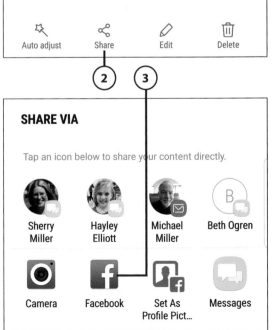

4 Say something about this photo, if you want.

5 Tap Share to post the photo as a status update.

Uploading from the Gallery

You can also upload photos you've taken previously, from your phone's picture gallery. Just navigate to and open the photo you want to post, tap Share, and proceed from there.

Shoot with a Filter or Effect

In addition to posting normal photos as part of a post, Facebook enables you to shoot a selfie with your phone with special effects and filters added. These filters are similar to the filters in Snapchat, another photo-sharing app popular with younger users.

You can shoot a fun selfie directly from the Facebook mobile app, without first creating a status update.

1 In the Facebook mobile app, tap the camera icon at the top-left corner.

2 Tap Normal, and make sure your phone's front camera is selected. (If not, tap the "reverse" icon.)

3 Aim the phone's front-facing camera so your face is centered on-screen, and then tap the Magic Wand icon.

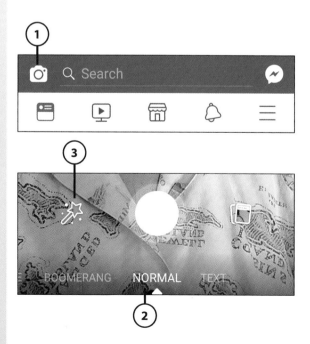

(4) Tap a type of filter on the bottom
row.

(5) Tap a filter or effect to apply it.
You can see the result onscreen.

(6) Tap the big round Camera button
to shoot the photo.

(7) Tap Next to display the Share
Photo page.

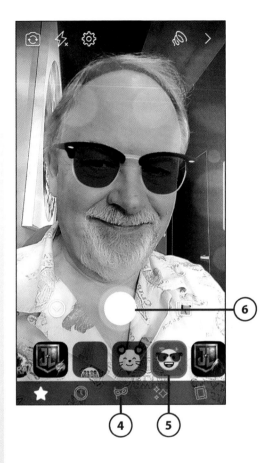

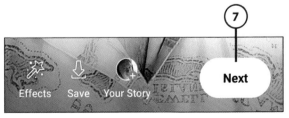

8) Tap Your Story if you want to share this with your Facebook Story.

9) Tap Post to share as a post to your friends.

10) Tap the name of a group to share this photo to a group of which you're a member.

11) Tap the Post button to post this picture to your News Feed.

Upload Photos to a New Photo Album

If you have a lot of photos to share on Facebook, the best approach is to create a series of virtual photo albums. This enables you to organize your photos by topic or date. For example, you might create an album for Summer Vacation, Thanksgiving, Grandkids, or Retirement Party. Organizing your photos into albums also makes it easier for your friends to find specific photos.

This task is most easily done on the Facebook website, from your computer.

1) From your profile page, click Photos to display your Photos page.

2) Click the Create Album button to display the Open dialog box.

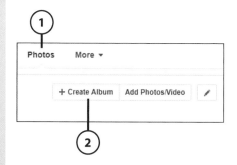

3 Select the photo(s) you want to upload.

4 Click the Open button to see the Untitled Album page.

Selecting Multiple Photos

It's easy to upload more than one photo at a time. Just hold down the Ctrl key while clicking files to select multiple files.

5 Click Album Name and enter the desired album title. (Note that this page looks slightly different in different browsers; I'm showing it in Google Chrome.)

6 Click Description and enter an album description.

7 Enter a location in the Location box to enter a geographic location for all the photos in this album. (You can later change the location for any specific photo, as noted in step 12.)

8 Check the High Quality option to upload these photos at a quality suitable for printing. Leave this box unchecked if the photos will only be viewed onscreen.

9 In the Change Date section, opt to either Use Date from Photos (each photo retains the date when it taken) or Pick a Date (to have all photos you're uploading have the same date).

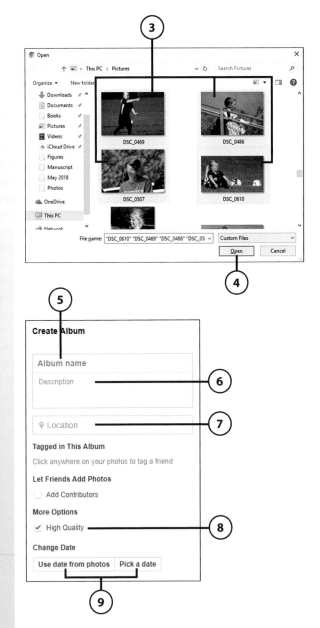

Optional Information

All the information you can add to a photo album is entirely optional; you can add as much or as little as you like. You don't even have to add a title— if you don't, Facebook uses the title Untitled Album.

High-Quality Photos

For best possible picture quality for anyone downloading or printing your photos, check the High Quality option to upload and store your photos at their original resolution. Note, however, that it takes longer to upload high-quality photos than those in standard quality.

(10) To enter information about a specific picture, enter a description in the Say Something About This Photo box for that photo.

(11) Click the Settings (gear) icon and select Change Date to enter when this photo was taken.

(12) If you want to enter a location for a specific photo that's different from the location you set for the entire album, click the Settings icon and select Edit Location.

(13) To tag a person in a given photo, click that person's face and enter his or her name when prompted.

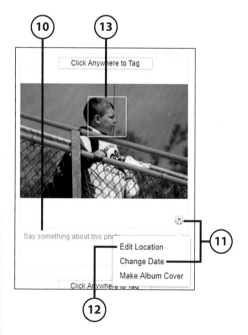

Click Anywhere to Tag

Say something about this photo

Edit Location
Change Date
Make Album Cover

Click Anywhere to Tag

Photo Tagging

You identify people in your photos by *tagging* them—that is, you click a person in the photo and then assign a friend's name to that part of the photo. You can then find photos where a given person appears by searching for that person's tag.

(14) Click the Privacy button and make a selection—Public, Friends, Friends Except, Only Me, or More—to determine who can view the photos in this album.

(15) Click the Post button.

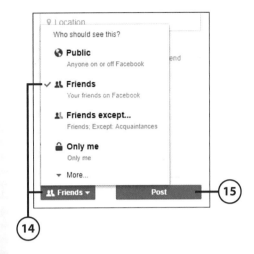

Upload More Photos to an Existing Photo Album

After you've created a photo album, you can easily upload more photos to that album.

(1) From your Photos page, click Albums to display your existing photo albums.

(2) Click the album to which you want to add new photos.

(3) When the album page opens, click + Add Photos/Videos to display the Open dialog box.

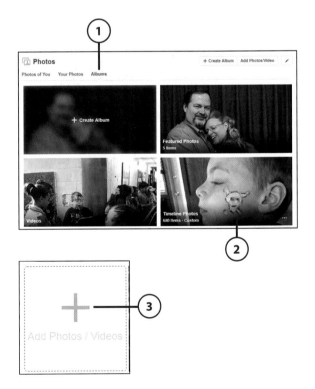

4 Navigate to and select the photo(s) to upload.

5 Click the Open button.

6 When the next page appears, you see the new photo(s) you've chosen to upload. You can enter an optional description for each picture in the Say Something About This Photo box.

7 To change the default location or date, click the Settings icon and select either Edit Location or Change Date. (You can also click a person's face to tag that individual.)

8 Click the Post button. The new photos are now added to the existing album.

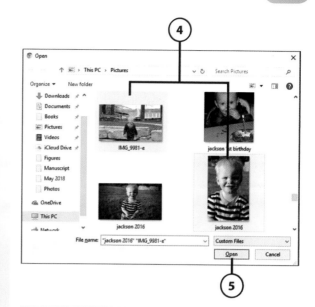

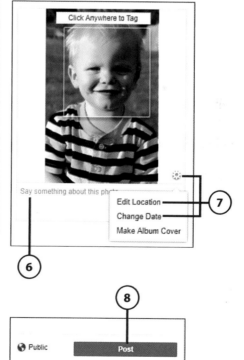

Delete a Photo

If you later discover that you've uploaded a photo you don't want to share, Facebook lets you delete individual photos within an album.

1. From the Facebook website, display the photo you want to delete, mouse over the photo to display the bottom menu, and then click Options to display the pop-up menu.

2. Click Delete This Photo; then click Confirm when prompted.

3. In the Facebook mobile app, display the photo you want to delete; then tap the More icon.

4. Tap Delete Photo.

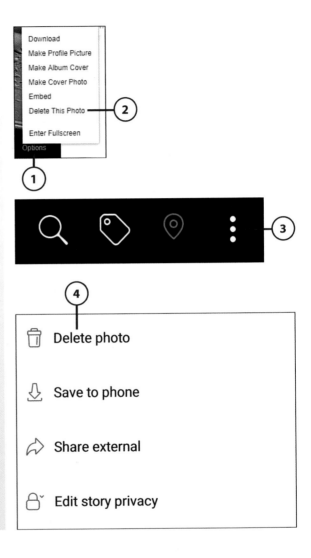

It's Not All Good

Deletion Is Final

When you delete a photo on Facebook, there's no way of undeleting that photo. You can, however, re-upload the photo to the album from scratch.

When you delete a photo album, not only is the deletion final, but you also delete all the photos within that album. Make sure you really want to delete a photo or album before you proceed.

Share a YouTube Video

In addition to uploading your own home videos, you can upload videos you find on YouTube (www.youtube.com), which is the world's largest online video community. Many Facebook users like to share videos they find on the YouTube site with their Facebook friends. Fortunately, both YouTube and Facebook make it easy to do this.

YouTube Account

To share YouTube videos, you first must have either a YouTube or a Google account. Both are free.

1. From the YouTube site or app (on your mobile device), navigate to the video you want to post to Facebook.

2. Tap or click Share.

3. Tap or click the Facebook icon.

4. Enter an accompanying message, if you want.

5. Tap or click the Privacy button (in the mobile app, the down arrow) to determine who can view this video.

6. Tap Post or click Post to Facebook. The video is posted as a status update to your Facebook timeline.

Linking Accounts

The first time you try to share a YouTube video on Facebook, you see the Facebook Login window. Enter your email address and Facebook password, and then click the Login button. (You won't see this window after the first time.)

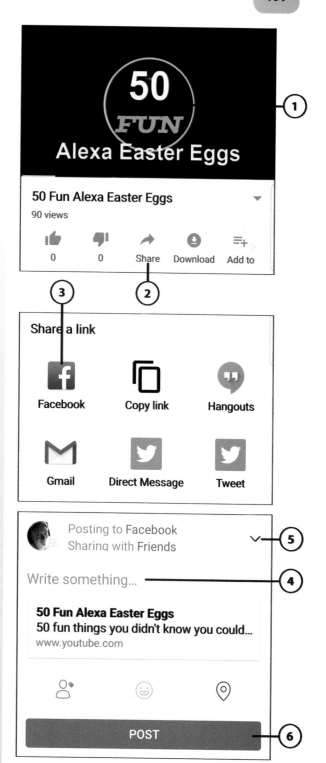

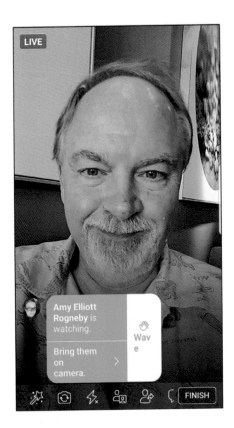
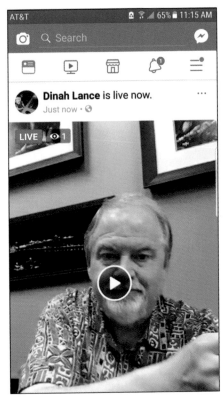

Facebook Live lets you broadcast live video of whatever you're doing at the time. In this chapter, you learn how to shoot Facebook Live videos—and watch videos shot by your Facebook friends.

Broadcasting Live with Facebook Live

Both the iOS and Android mobile apps let you share live video with your friends and others on Facebook. (You can also broadcast from the Facebook website, using your computer's webcam.) That means you can broadcast your own online shows from the comfort of your home or business—or wherever you happen to be.

Facebook Live videos are streamed in real time as you shoot them. Friends and family can "tune in" to see your live broadcast, or you can save the live video for others to view later. It's great for posting live from sporting events, birthday parties, or even work conferences...you name it.

Shooting a Live Video

Many people use Facebook Live to show their friends and families what they're doing at the moment, whether that is having lunch with friends, attending a grandchild's school concert or sports game, or just walking down the street and talking. Organizations use Facebook Live to broadcast live events, such as meetings, concerts, and the like.

Since Facebook Live videos can be up to four hours long, you can broadcast that entire football game or birthday party or conference—you have all the time you need. For example, my church recently did a four hour-long Facebook Live event to showcase all the people and services offered; I got to play live with the band for everyone to watch online!

Broadcast on Facebook Live

Shooting a live video for Facebook Live with your phone or tablet is much like shooting any video. Aim, press the big button, and off you go.

The difference with Facebook Live, of course, is that once you start shooting, you're completely live. Everything you shoot goes out live over Facebook until you stop shooting. It's all done in real time, with no opportunity to stop and reshoot or correct mistakes. It's live!

We'll examine how to use Facebook Live on the Facebook mobile app. You also can shoot with your computer's webcam, from the Facebook website—just start a new post and click Live Video. After that, the steps are similar to those listed here.

(1) From the Facebook mobile app, tap the Publisher box to start a new post.

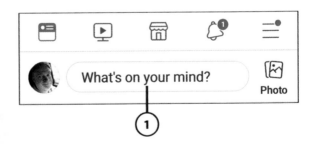

(2) Tap Go Live.

(3) The front-facing (selfie) camera on your phone now activates. If you want to shoot with your normal rear-facing camera, tap the reverse camera icon. (You don't have this option if you're shooting from your computer's webcam.)

(4) Tap to select the privacy level for your video—Public, Friends, and so forth.

(5) Enter a description of your video.

(6) Tap to select a theme for your video. (The default Live Video theme works best for most people.)

(7) Tap Start Live Video. Video recording starts, and an alert is sent to your Facebook friends, notifying them of the live event. The live video also shows in your friends' News Feeds.

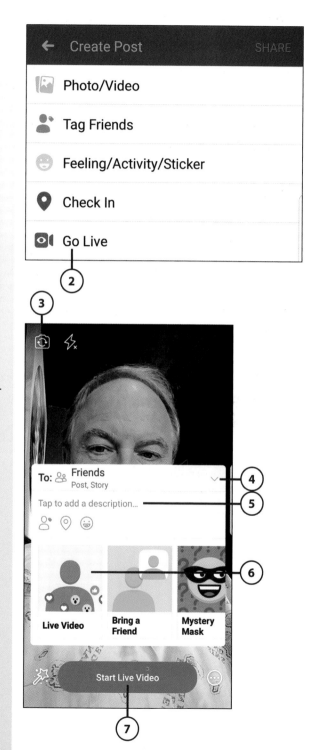

8 You are now broadcasting; note the red LIVE icon at the top of the screen. The screen itself shows what your viewers see.

9 Viewer's likes and comments appear at the bottom of the screen. You also see when new viewers join your broadcast.

10 Tap the magic wand icon to add a filter to your video.

11 Tap the reverse camera icon to switch from front-facing to rear-facing camera, or vice versa.

12 Tap the Flash icon to turn on or off your camera's flash.

13 Tap the Your Viewers icon to add viewers to your video.

14 Tap the Invite Friends icon to invite selected friends to your video.

15 Tap the Comment icon to add your own comments to the video.

16 When you're done shooting, tap Finish.

(17) You're prompted to post your formerly live video as a normal video to Facebook. Tap the privacy button to determine who can see this video replay.

(18) By default, this video is added to your Facebook Story. Uncheck this option if you don't want this.

(19) By default, this video is added to your Timeline. Uncheck this option if you don't want this.

(20) By default, this video is uploaded in high definition (HD). Uncheck this option if you'd rather upload in standard definition.

(21) Tap Delete if you don't want to post or save this video.

(22) Tap Save to save this video to your device.

(23) Tap Share to post this video.

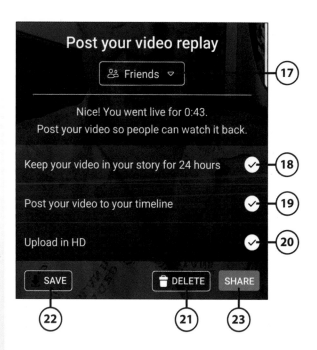

Watching a Facebook Live Video

Facebook Live videos stream live to anyone who wants to view it—depending on the privacy level the user has set, of course. When the live broadcast is over, the complete video is typically saved and posted to the person's profile page. If the privacy level was set to Friends or Public, it then shows up in all that person's friends' News Feeds, so they can watch that "live" broadcast after the fact. It's kind of like a Facebook rerun.

Watch a Live Video Live

A friend's live video should appear in your News Feed and on your friend's profile page as it happens.

1. If the live video appears in your News Feed, tap to watch it.

2. You also can access a live video from your friend's profile page. Open the profile page and scroll to the live video; then tap it to watch it.

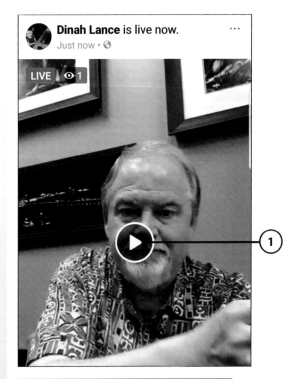

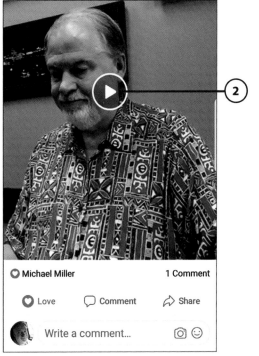

(3) While you're watching, comments from viewers appear at the bottom of the screen.

(4) Click or tap one of the Like icons to like the video.

(5) Tap or click Write a Comment to add a comment to this video.

(6) You don't have to watch the whole video, of course. Simply click or tap away from the video, or tap the back button on your mobile device to do something else. (Not shown.)

Watch a Live Video Rerun

After a live video is over, you may still be able to watch it—if your friend has saved the video. In this instance, the video has been recorded and is available from your friend's profile page (and sometimes in your News Feed, as well).

(1) Go to your friend's profile page, select Photos, select Albums, select Videos, and then tap to play the recorded video.

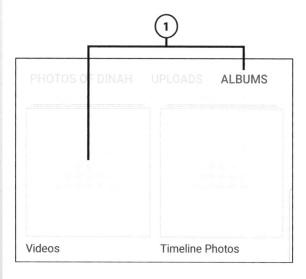

(**2**) While you're watching, comments from viewers appear at the bottom (app) or right side (website) of the screen.

(**3**) Tap or click a Like icon to express your feelings at that moment.

(**4**) Tap or click Write a Comment to add a comment to this video.

(**5**) When you're done watching, click or tap away from the video, or tap the back button on your mobile device to do something else. (Not shown.)

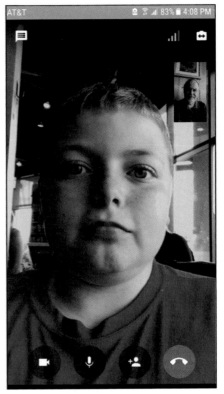

In this chapter, you find out how to use Facebook Messenger to chat privately with other Facebook users.

→ Exchanging Text Messages on the Facebook Website
→ Mobile Messaging with the Messenger App
→ Video Chatting on Facebook

12

Chatting with Facebook Messenger

Facebook is a public social network, which means it encourages public interaction between you and your friends. But you might not want all your communications to be public; sometimes you just want to send a private message to someone you know.

That's why, in addition to its public status updates, Facebook lets you send private messages to your Facebook friends. You also can use Facebook to conduct video chats, so you speak face-to-face with friends and family.

On your mobile device, you do all this with a separate Facebook Messenger app. (You need to download this free app to your phone or tablet.) Messenger is incorporated into the Facebook website.

Exchanging Text Messages on the Facebook Website

Facebook lets any user send private text messages to any other user. These messages don't appear on either person's News Feed or profile page; it's the Facebook equivalent of private email.

If you're using Facebook on your computer, you can send and receive text messages on the Facebook website, using your web browser. (If you're using Facebook on your phone or tablet, skip to the "Mobile Messaging with the Messenger App" section, later in this chapter.)

Send a Text Message

Sending a private text message to another Facebook user is as easy as sending an email to that person—even easier, actually. Your master Facebook friends list functions much as a contacts list in an email program; you can add recipients to a message just by typing a few letters of their name.

(1) Click Messages in the toolbar.

(2) Click See All in Messenger (at the bottom of the menu) to display the Messages page.

(3) Click the New Message button to display the New Message panel.

4 Enter the name of the recipient into the To box.

5 As you type, Facebook displays matching friends; select the desired recipient from the list.

6 Enter your message into the Type a Message box.

7 Attach a photo to this message by clicking Add Photos and selecting the photo you want.

8 Click any of the other icons to add a sticker, GIF, emoji, or other items to your message.

9 Press Enter or click the Send button to send the message on its way.

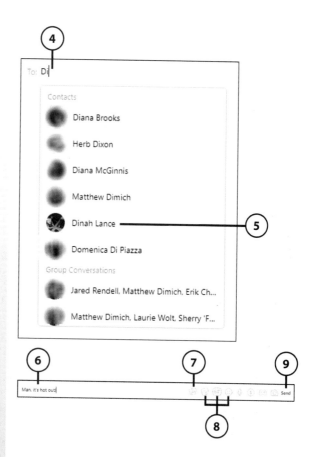

Read a Message

When you receive a new private message from a friend, you see a red number on top of the Messages icon on the Facebook toolbar. Click the Messages icon to read all your new private messages. Better yet, open the separate Messages page to view all your private messages—new and old.

1 Click the Messages button in the Facebook toolbar to view your most recent messages.

2 Click any message snippet to view the entire message in a separate message pane.

3 All your messages to and from this person are displayed in the form of a flowing conversation. The newest messages are at the bottom of the pane.

4 To respond to this person's latest message, enter your message into the bottom text box and press Enter.

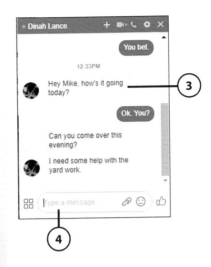

Live Chat

If the person you're messaging is online at the same time you are, your private messages become a live text chat. Your friend sees your messages in real time, and you see her replies immediately, as well.

View All Messages

Clicking the Messages button on the toolbar only displays your most recent messages. You can view all messages you've received on the Messages page.

1 On the Facebook toolbar, click the Messages button to display the menu of messages and options.

2 Click See All in Messenger at the bottom of the menu to open the Messages panel.

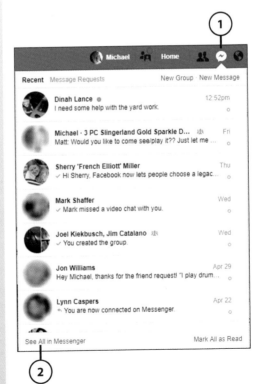

3 All messages are in a scrolling list on the left side of the page. Click a message to view all messages to and from that person in the center section of the page.

4 To reply to the current message, enter your text into the Type a Message box at the bottom of the page.

5 Click the Send button.

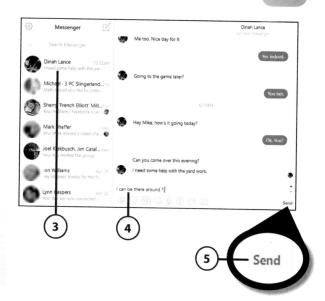

Mobile Messaging with the Messenger App

If you want to send and receive private text messages from your smartphone or tablet, you can't do it from the Facebook mobile app. Instead, you need to use a separate app, called Facebook Messenger, to do this sort of instant messaging. Like the regular Facebook app, the Messenger app is free for downloading for both Apple and Android devices.

The Facebook Messenger app does more than just connect you with your Facebook friends, however. If you opt for the default installation, the Messenger app taps into your phone's contacts list and identifies those contacts who are also on Facebook. This means that you can instant message with any of your contacts who are also Facebook users, even if they're not currently on your friends list.

Note that the Messenger app looks a little different on Android devices than it does on your iPhone or iPad; in particular, the navigation icons are on the bottom in the iOS app, and on the top in the Android app. I'm showing the Android version of this app for the examples, but the same functionality exists on the iOS version.

Send and Receive Text Messages

Just like the Facebook website does, Messenger enables you to send and receive either real-time text messages or private email-like messages. If the person you want to talk to is online, you communicate in real-time text chat. If the person you want to talk to is not currently online, you send that person a private text message instead.

1. Open the Messenger app and tap the Home icon.

2. Tap the Messages tab to view a list of your most recent text conversations and private messages.

3. Tap a conversation header to view messages between you and that person.

4. To continue the conversation, tap within the Type a Message box and then use your phone's onscreen keyboard to type a message.

5. Tap Send to send the message to the other person.

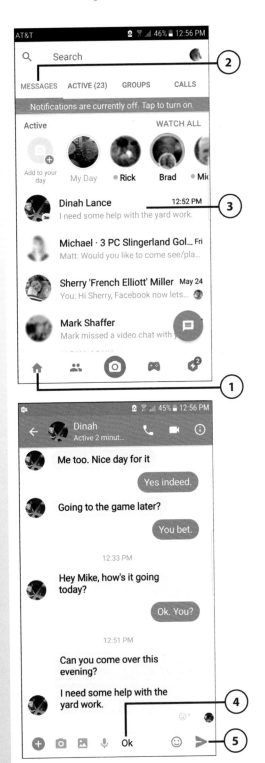

6 Create a new text message by tapping the New Message icon.

7 Your favorite contacts are listed on this screen. Tap a person's name or picture to begin the conversation. *Or...*

8 Enter a person's name into the Search box at the top of the screen and then tap the person you want from the search results.

9 Enter your message into the Type a Message box.

10 Tap the Camera icon to take and send a photo.

11 Tap the Photos icon to send a photo stored in your phone's gallery.

12 Tap the Emoji icon to insert an emoji, GIF, or sticker into your message.

13 Tap Send to send the message.

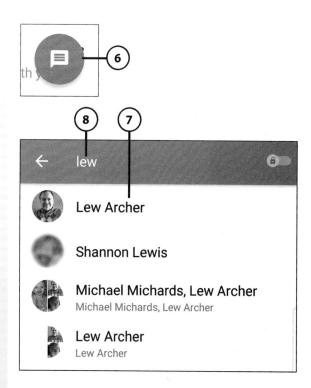

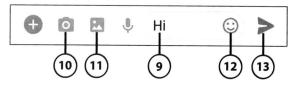

>>>*Go Further*

MESSAGING FROM THE CONTACTS SCREEN

You can also send messages directly from Messenger's Contacts screen. Tap the Contacts or People icon to display a list of your Facebook friends. Select the Messenger tab to view friends who have the Messenger app installed; select the Active tab to view friends who are currently online and available to chat. (Friends using Messenger and currently online have a green dot next to their pictures.) Tap a person's name to start the conversation.

Use Chat Heads

When you have the Messenger app installed on your Android phone, the profile picture of anyone with whom you've been chatting appears as a round bubble called a chat head. (Chat heads are not available on Apple devices or the Facebook website.) Chat heads float above all your other active apps on your phone, constantly reminding you that you have an open chat session running in the background. You can move chat heads anywhere on the screen; just tap and drag them from place to place.

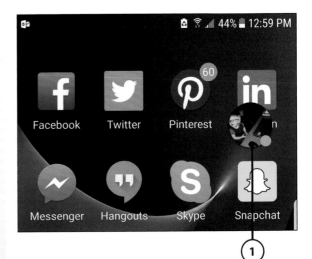

① Tap a chat head to reopen a conversation with that person.

② This conversation floats above the other apps on your phone. Enter your message into the Type a Message box.

3 Tap and drag a chat head to the X at the bottom of the screen to close the conversation and make the chat head go away.

>>>Go Further
PHONE CALLS AND VIDEO CHATS

If the person you're messaging with is in your phone's contacts list, or if that person's phone number is listed with Facebook, you can turn your text message into a phone call. From within any conversation, tap the telephone icon to place the call.

You can also turn any text conversation into a video chat. From within any conversation, tap the Video Camera icon to begin a video chat.

Create a Group Conversation

The Messenger app isn't just for one-on-one conversations. You can also participate in group chats.

1. Within the Messenger app, tap the Groups tab to display the Groups page.

2. Any groups you've previously communicated with are displayed here. Tap a group to open a new conversation with that group.

3. Tap the + button to create a new group.

4. Tap to select the names of people you want to include in this group.

5. Tap the Create Group (right arrow) button.

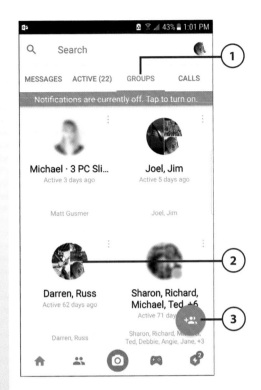

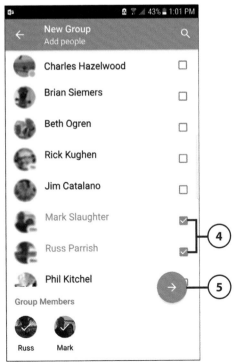

6 The new group appears on the Groups page. Tap the group to open that group's conversation page.

7 To name the group, tap Name Group and enter a name.

8 To send a message to the group, enter your text into the Type a Message box.

9 Tap any of the other icons to send to the group a photo, emoji, voice message, or sticker.

10 Tap Send to send the message. Your message and messages from other group members appear in the center of the screen.

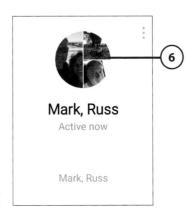

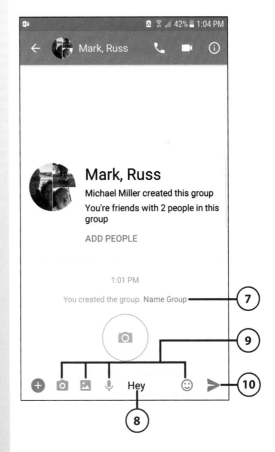

Video Chatting on Facebook

In addition to text messaging, Facebook lets you talk to other Facebook users face-to-face via video chat. Video chatting is a great way to get up-close and personal with distant family and friends; you can see them and they can see you.

You can chat from your mobile phone or tablet using the device's front-facing camera. You can also chat from a desktop or notebook computer, assuming it has a webcam built-in or attached.

Chat from the Messenger App

If you're connecting to Facebook from your mobile phone or tablet, you use the Messenger app to do your video chatting. You can chat with other phone and tablet users or with users connecting to Facebook from their computers (assuming they have a webcam connected to their computer, of course).

1. From within the Messenger app, tap the Calls tab to display the Calls page.

2. Friends who have video cameras are displayed with a blue video camera icon. Tap the video camera icon for the friend with whom you want to chat.

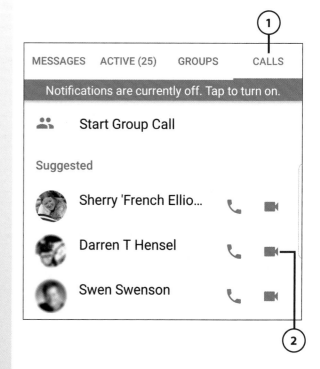

3 When your friend answers the call, you see his picture on your device's screen, and the video chat begins.

4 Your picture appears smaller in the corner.

5 Tap the red hang up button to end the video chat.

Video Chat from a Text Chat
You also can switch to a video chat from within a text chat. Just tap the Video icon at the top of the text chat screen to open a video chat with the same person.

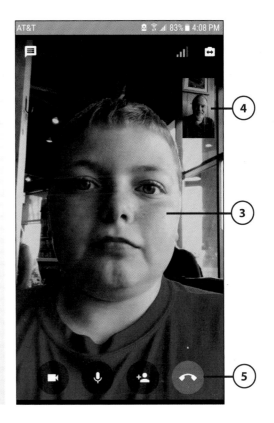

Chat from the Facebook Website

You can also engage in video chats from your desktop or notebook computer. Most notebook computers have a built-in web camera (webcam); you may need to connect an external webcam to a desktop PC.

Install the Chat Applet
The first time you use Facebook's video chat, you're prompted to download and install the necessary background chat applet on your computer. (An applet is a small application that runs in the background—in this case, to enable video chat.) Follow the onscreen instructions to do so.

1 Click the Chat gadget at the bottom-right corner of any Facebook page to display the full Chat panel. (If your web browser is wide enough, you'll see the Chat panel already displayed as a fourth column onscreen.)

2 Click the name of the friend you want to chat with to open an individual Chat panel with the selected friend.

3 If your friend has a webcam and is available to chat, you'll see a camera icon at the top of the Chat panel. Click this Start a Video Chat button to initiate the video chat.

(4) When your friend answers the call, Facebook displays the video chat window. Your friend appears in the main part of the window.

(5) Your picture is in a smaller window in the corner of the screen.

(6) When you're ready to close the chat, mouse over the chat window and then click the red End Call button.

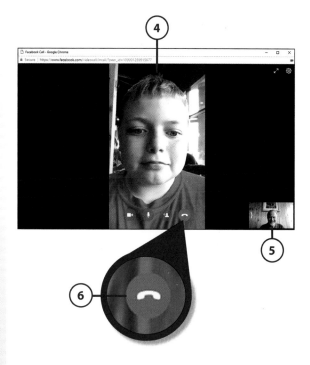

Webcams and Microphones

Most webcams (whether attached or built into your computer) also have built-in microphones. The camera in the webcam captures your picture, and the microphone in the webcam captures your voice. Just speak into the webcam to talk during a video chat.

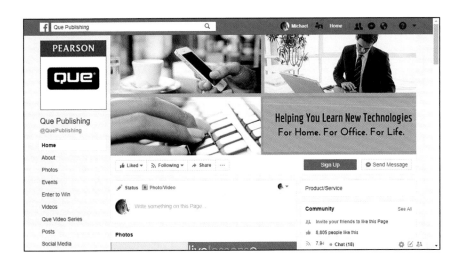

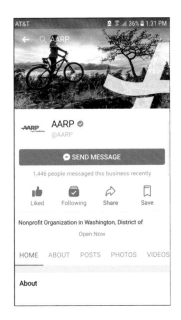

In this chapter, you find out how to follow companies and public figures on Facebook.

→ Finding and Following Companies and Public Figures
→ Managing the Pages You Follow

Liking Pages from Companies and Public Figures

Regular people on Facebook have their own profile pages. Businesses and public figures on Facebook, however, have their own special pages that are kind of like profile pages but different; they're tailored for the needs of customers and fans. These pages—rather unimaginatively called *Facebook Pages, with a capital "P"*—are how you keep abreast of what your favorite brands, products, and famous people are up to.

Finding and Following Companies and Public Figures

Even though businesses, celebrities, and public figures aren't regular users, they still want to use Facebook to connect with their customers and fans. They do this through Facebook Pages—essentially profile pages for companies and public figures. If you're a fan of a given company or celebrity, you can "like" that entity's Facebook Page—and keep abreast of what that company or individual is up to. It's kind of like joining an online fan club through Facebook.

Search for Companies and Public Figures

Many companies and organizations have Facebook Pages for their brands and the products they sell. For example, you can find and follow Pages for AARP, McDonald's, Starbucks, Walmart, and similar entities.

Many famous people—entertainers, athletes, news reporters, politicians, and the like—also have Facebook Pages. So if you're a fan of Ellen DeGeneres, Sean Hannity, LeBron James, James Taylor, or Oprah Winfrey, you can follow any or all of them via their Facebook pages.

(1) Enter one or more keywords that describe the person, company, or organization into the Search box. As you type, Facebook displays a list of Pages and people that match your query.

(2) If the Page you want is listed, tap or click it. If the Page you want is not listed, press Enter or tap the See Results link. You now see more results.

(3) Click or tap the Pages tab.

(4) You now see all Pages related to your search. Click or tap the name of the Page you want to view.

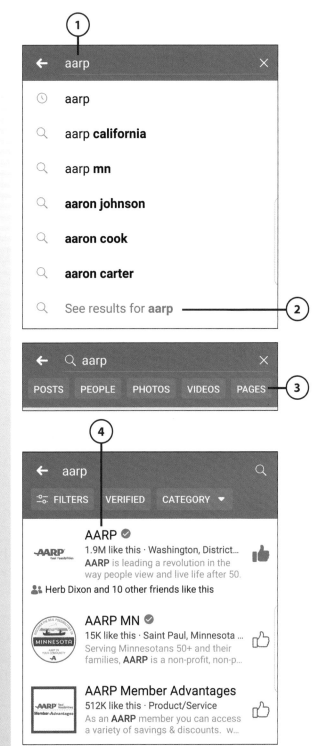

>>>Go Further

WHO GETS OR HAS A PAGE?

Just about any public person or entity can create a Facebook Page. You can create Facebook Pages for businesses, brands, and products; for musicians, actors, and other celebrities; for politicians, public servants, and other public figures; and for school classes, public organizations, special events, and social causes.

If you want to create your own Page for your business or community organization, tap the More icon at the top of the Facebook app screen, tap Pages, and then tap + Create. (On the Facebook website, click the down arrow on the toolbar and then click Create Page.) From there, follow the onscreen instructions. To create a Page, you must be an official representative of the group or company behind the page; fans can't create official Pages for the companies and entertainers they follow.

View and Like a Facebook Page

A professional Facebook Page is very similar to a personal profile page, right down to the timeline of updates and activities. Pages can feature specialized content, however, which is located at the top of the Page, under the cover image. For example, a musician's Page might feature an audio player for that performer's songs; other Pages might let you view pictures and videos or even purchase items online.

Note that a celebrity or company on Facebook can't be your friend; that is, you can't add a professional Page to your Facebook friends list. Instead, you can choose to like that Page so that you can follow posts made by that entity. Unlike when you friend an individual, the Pages you like do not reciprocate and follow all the status updates that you make on a regular basis.

Liking

Liking a Page is a one-way thing. When you like a Page you follow that Page, but that Page doesn't follow you.

(1) Click or tap Like to like and follow the posts on this Page.

(2) Click About to read more about this person or company.

(3) Click Photos to view the Page's official pictures.

(4) Click any other content to view that content.

(5) Scroll down to view status updates and other postings.

>>>Go Further

PROMOTED VERSUS ORGANIC POSTS

Facebook used to display all posts from those Pages you like in your News Feed. It doesn't do that anymore. That's because Facebook is in the business of making money, and one way it does that is to charge companies to "promote" their page posts.

When a post is promoted (that is, paid for), Facebook displays it in the News Feeds of that Page's followers. If a post is not promoted, Facebook probably won't display that post in anyone's News Feeds. If a company wants its followers to see its posts, it pretty much has to pay for that privilege.

Although some nonpromoted posts may show up in your News Feed from time to time, Facebook displays less than 20% of a Page's "organic" (non-paid) posts. In other words, signing up to like a given Page does not guarantee that you'll see all (or even most) of the posts to that Page. If you want to see all that a company or person is posting, you have to go to that Page to read the posts directly.

Managing the Pages You Follow

Some people only follow a handful of professional Facebook Pages. Others find dozens of Pages to follow. If you're a more prolific follower, you might want to manage your Pages list over time.

View Your Favorite Pages

Not sure of which Pages exactly you're following? Then it's time to display all your favorite Facebook pages, in the Pages list. This is easiest done on the Facebook website.

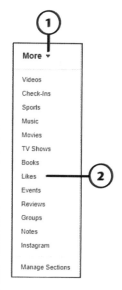

(1) From your profile page, click More under your cover image.

(2) Select Likes to display those Pages you've liked.

(3) Click any given image to display that specific Page.

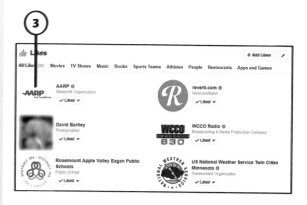

Unlike a Page

Just because you liked a given company or celebrity at one point in time doesn't mean you'll continue to like that entity forever. Your tastes change, after all, or you might find you don't like the posts a given Page is making.

When you find yourself not liking a Page so much, you can "unlike" that page. Unliking a Page ensures you won't receive any more status updates or notifications from it.

To unlike a Page, start by opening that Page, either in the Facebook mobile app or on the Facebook website.

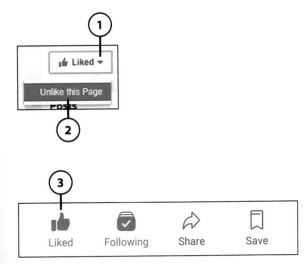

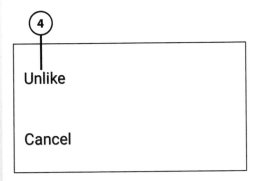

1. On the Facebook website, mouse over the Liked button.

2. Click Unlike This Page. *Or...*

3. In the mobile app, tap Liked.

4. Tap Unlike.

Re-Liking

You can always re-like an unliked page in the future. Just repeat the steps in the "View and Like a Facebook Page" section, earlier in this chapter, to like the page, and you'll be following it again.

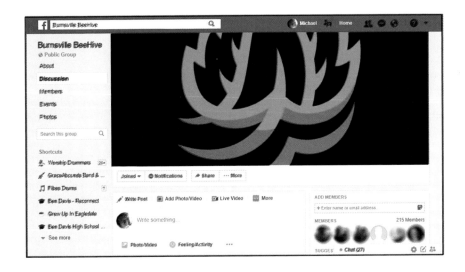

In this chapter, you find out how to find and participate in interesting Facebook groups.

→ Finding and Joining Facebook Groups
→ Working with Facebook Groups
→ Using Groups to Reconnect with Old Friends

Participating in Interesting Facebook Groups

As you read in the previous chapter, Facebook Pages are like fan clubs for companies and celebrities and other public figures. There are other kinds of "clubs" on Facebook, however, in the form of public *groups*. Facebook has groups for all types of interests.

Many of you are probably interested in groups that reunite you with people you've known in the past. These could be groups devoted to your old town or neighborhood, your old grade school or high school, or even activities you used to participate in. These groups are great ways to reminisce about the old times and keep in touch with people you knew back then.

Finding and Joining Facebook Groups

If you want to make new friends—and reconnect with old ones—one of the best ways to do so is to search out others who share your interests. If you're into gardening, look for gardeners. If you're into recreational vehicles, look for fellow RVers. If you're a wine lover, look for other connoisseurs of the grape.

Even better, look for people who've shared your life experiences. That means connecting with people who went to the same schools, lived in the same neighborhoods, and participated in the same activities.

You can find people who share your history and hobbies in Facebook groups. A group takes the form of a special Facebook page, a place for people interested in that topic to meet online and exchange information and pleasantries.

Find a Group

Facebook offers hundreds of thousands of different groups online, so chances are you can find one or more that suit you. The key is finding a particular group that matches what you're interested in—which you do by searching.

(1) On the Facebook website, click the down arrow on the toolbar, and then click Your Groups. (Alternatively, click Groups in the Explore section of the navigation column.) Then skip to step 4.

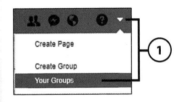

(2) In the Facebook mobile app, tap the More button, and then tap Groups.

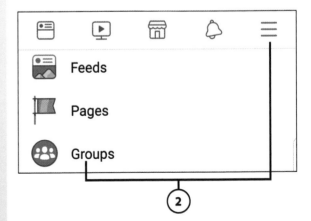

3 In the mobile app, tap the Discover tab.

4 The Recommended or Recommended Groups section displays groups Facebook thinks you'll like. Tap or click a group name to view that group's page.

5 Tap or click Join to join the group.

6 Tap or click another tab at the top to view different types of recommended groups—Recent Interest, Sports, Games, and so forth.

7 To search for a specific type of group, enter one or more keywords that describe what you're looking for into the search box at the top of the page. For example, if you're interested in sewing, enter **sewing**. If you're looking for a group for graduates from your high school, enter *high school name* **alumni**. (Replace *high school name* with the name of your high school, of course.) If you want to find a group created by people who live on the west side of Indianapolis, enter **Indianapolis west side**.

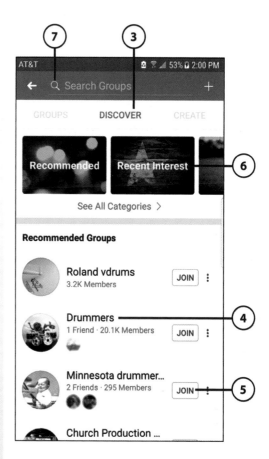

Join a Group

After you find a group, you can offi-
cially join it—and then participate to
whatever degree suits your fancy. You
can join a group from the Discover
Groups page or from the group's
Facebook page.

1 To join a group from the Discover
Groups page, tap or click the Join
button. *Or…*

2 To join a group from its Facebook
page, tap or click Join Group.

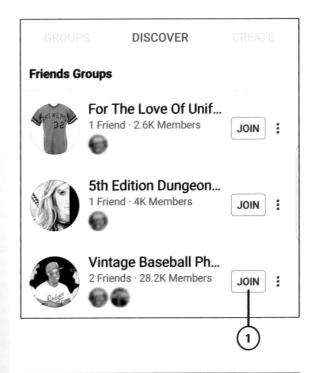

>>>*Go Further*

PUBLIC AND CLOSED GROUPS

Most groups are classified as Public groups, meaning they're open for all Facebook members to join. Some groups, however, are Closed groups, which require that the group administrator approve all requests for membership.

To join a Closed group, you must apply for membership and hope that your request is granted. When you click the Join or Join Group button, a request goes to the group administrator. If your request is granted, you receive a message that you've been approved and are now an official member of the group. If your request is not granted, you don't get a response.

Working with Facebook Groups

What can you do in a Facebook group? A lot, actually. You can read the latest news, discover new information, view photos and movies, exchange messages with other group members, and engage in online discussions about the topic at hand. It's just like participating in a real-world club, except you do it all on Facebook.

Visit a Group Page

Although you can view a feed of messages from all your groups (covered later in this chapter), most people prefer to visit individual group pages. This enables you to partake in all of the resources available in a given group.

1. In the Facebook mobile app, tap the More button and then tap Groups. *Or...*

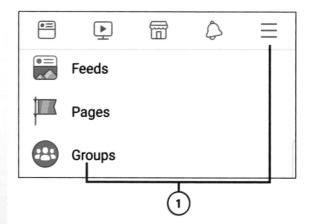

2 On the Facebook website, go to your home page, scroll down the navigation sidebar to the Explore section, and click Groups. This displays the Groups page with the Groups tab selected.

3 Click or tap the name of a group to open its Facebook page.

Read and Reply to Posts

After you open a group page, you can read posts from other members of the group and then like and comment on those posts as you would normal Facebook status updates.

Group Posts

Posts that you make on a group's Facebook page may be displayed only on that page, not in individual members' News Feeds, depending on their Facebook settings.

1 Open the group's page and tap or click the Discussion tab.

2 Scroll down to the Recent Activity section to view recent posts from group members.

3 Click or tap Like to like a particular post.

4 Click or tap Comment to reply to a post and then enter your reply into the Write a Comment box.

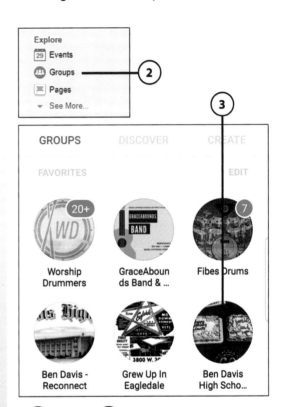

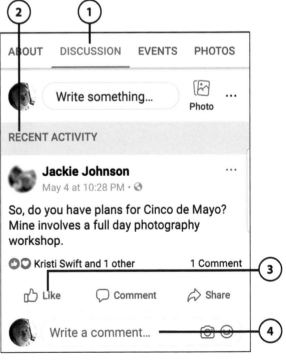

Create a New Group Post

Not only can you reply to posts made by other members, you can start a new discussion by creating a new post on the group's page. Other group members can then like and reply to your message.

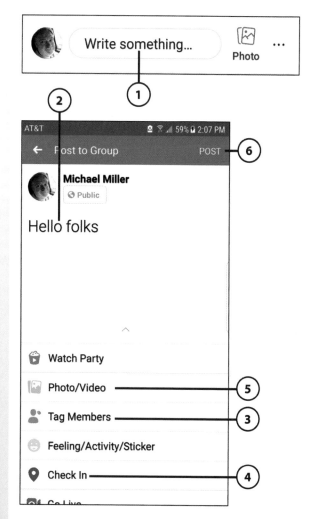

(1) Open the group's page, navigate to the Discussion tab, and then click or tap within the Publisher (Write Something) box; the box expands.

(2) Type your post into the Write Something or What's On Your Mind? section.

(3) Click Tag Friends or tap Tag Members to tag another group member in this post.

(4) Click or tap Check In to add a location to this post.

(5) Click or tap Photo/Video to add photographs or a video to this post.

(6) Click or tap Post to post your message to the group.

Get Notified of Group Activity

If you're active in a Facebook group, you might want to be notified when others post to the group. You can opt to receive notifications of each post made, or only of those posts made by your friends.

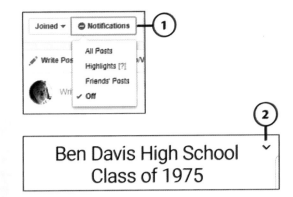

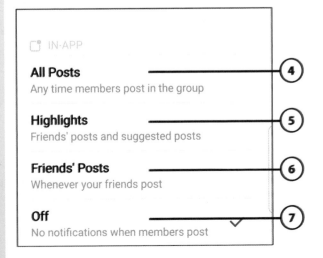

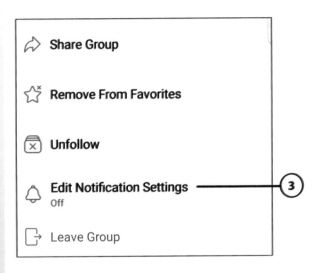

(1) On the Facebook website, open the group's page and click Notifications. *Or...*

(2) In the Facebook app, tap the down arrow next to the group's name.

(3) Tap Edit Notification Settings.

(4) Select All Posts to receive a notification whenever a post is made to the group.

(5) Select Highlights to receive notification of only friends posts and other important posts.

(6) Select Friends' Posts to receive a notification whenever one of your Facebook friends' posts to this group.

(7) Select Off to not receive any notifications from this group.

Leave a Group

If you grow tired of irrelevant or unin-teresting posts in a given group, you can choose to unsubscribe from or leave a group.

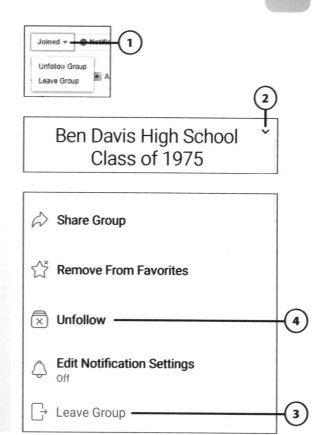

1. On the Facebook website, open the group's page and click the Joined button. *Or…*

2. In the mobile app, tap the down arrow next to the group's name.

3. Click or tap Leave Group to per-manently leave the group.

4. Click Unfollow Group or tap Unfollow to stay in the group but not see group posts in your News Feed.

Using Groups to Reconnect with Old Friends

Although there are a number of club-like Facebook groups, there are also groups that are more about times and places than they are about hobbies and interests. As such, these groups attempt to reconnect people with shared experiences.

For example, I grew up on the west side of Indianapolis, Indiana, and now I belong to a Facebook group called Growing Up on Indy's Westside. It's a fun little group, with people posting faded pictures of old haunts and having lots of dis-cussions about the way things used to be and what we used to do back then.

You might even meet up with some of your old friends in these groups, or make some new friends you should have made way back then. It's kind of a virtual blast from the past, and we have Facebook to thank for it.

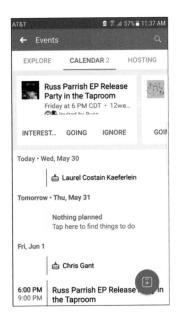

In this chapter, you find out how to respond to event notifications and schedule your own events on Facebook—as well as celebrate your friends' birthdays online.

→ Responding to Event Invitations
→ Scheduling a New Event
→ Celebrating Birthdays

Attending Events and Celebrating Birthdays

Facebook lets you do more than just post and read status updates to and from your friends and family. You can also use Facebook as a kind of event scheduler, so you can manage parties, meetings, reunions, and the like from within Facebook.

The most common type of event is a birthday, and Facebook helps out there, too. Facebook notifies you of your friends' and family members' upcoming birthdays and makes it easy for you to send your birthday greetings. Facebook even announces your birthday to your friends—so sit back and wait for those well wishes to arrive!

Responding to Event Invitations

You use Facebook to keep in touch with all your friends and family, so it's only natural to use Facebook to schedule events that might involve these same people. You're all online and on Facebook, after all; why not use Facebook to notify people of upcoming events?

Facebook's events feature lets you do just that—schedule events and invite your Facebook friends to those events, using Facebook's built-in messaging system. In effect, Facebook creates a new page for each event scheduled, and whoever creates the event can then invite people to view the page and attend the event. If you receive an invitation to a Facebook event, you can then decide to accept or decline the invitation.

Respond to an Invitation

When you've been invited to an event, you receive a notification about the event. Click the notification to view the Facebook page for that event and then let the host know whether you'll be attending.

No Obligation

You should feel no obligation to accept any specific event. Only accept those you genuinely want to and can attend.

1. On the Facebook website, event notifications are displayed near the top of the right column. (Depending on your notification settings, you also might receive a Facebook notification of the event.) Click X Event Invites to view recent invitations; then skip to Step 5.

2. In the Facebook mobile app, tap the More button.

3. Tap Events.

4. In the mobile app, tap the Calendar tab to view recent invitations.

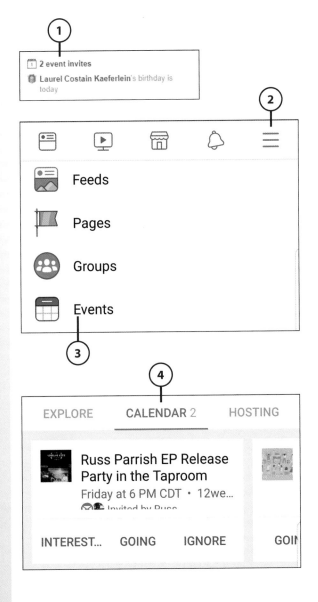

5 Click or tap the event notification to display the event page with more information about that event. *Or…*

6 Click or tap Going to accept the invitation.

7 Click or tap Interested or Maybe if you're not sure whether you'll attend.

8 Click or tap Ignore if you don't want to go to the event.

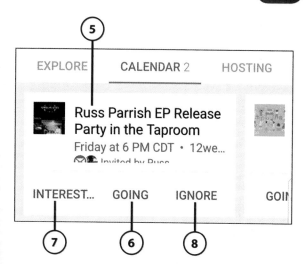

Find Nearby Events

You don't have to wait to be invited to an event; Facebook makes it easy to find events near your location. Just open the Events page (and, in the Android app, tap the Explore tab). Facebook now shows suggested events nearby. In the Android app, you can scroll down to see events by type. On the website, you can scroll down to see events your friends are attending, or click the links in the Find Events panel (on the right) to view events by type.

View an Event Page

When a friend schedules a new event, Facebook creates a page for that event. You can view the event page to learn more about the event.

1 Click or tap the name of an event to view the page for that event.

(2) Click or tap the appropriate option to tell the host whether you're going to this event.

(3) View information about the event, such as the date, time, and location.

(4) Click or tap the location to view more information about that venue.

(5) To see who's attending this event, scroll to and click or tap Going.

(6) Use the Publisher ("Say Something") box to post your own message to the people invited to this event.

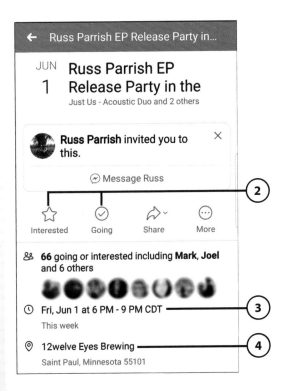

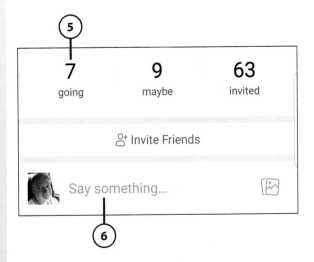

>>>*Go Further*

FACEBOOK EVENTS

What exactly is an event? On Facebook, an event is any item on your personal schedule. Events can be small and private, such as a doctor's appointment or dinner with a friend. Events can also be large and public, such as a community meeting or family reunion.

This means that you can use Facebook events to invite friends to backyard BBQs, block parties, golf dates, and card games. You can also use Facebook events to invite family members to birthday parties, holiday gatherings, and family reunions.

The events you create don't have to be real-world, physical events, either. You can schedule virtual events, such as inviting all your friends to watch a specific TV show or sporting event on a given evening. You can also schedule online events, such as seminars and conferences on sites that offer such options. In other words, you don't have to meet someone in person to share an event with them. It's all part of the social networking thing.

Scheduling a New Event

You don't have to wait to be invited to an event. You can schedule your own Facebook events.

Maybe your neighborhood association has a meeting coming up. Maybe you're hosting a house party for some friends. Or maybe you just want to let everyone know about an upcoming anniversary. Whatever the case, Facebook makes it relatively easy to create new events and invite some or all of your Facebook friends to these events.

Create an Event

Facebook lets you create all manner of events, from parties to community meetings, and invite selected friends to those events. You can then manage that event through the event's Facebook page.

We'll examine how to create an event from the Facebook website. The process is similar with the mobile app.

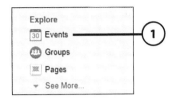

(1) On the Facebook website, click Events in the navigation sidebar; in the mobile app, tap More and then tap Events. This displays your Events page.

(2) Click or tap Create Event.

(3) By default, Facebook events are private—visible only to those who receive invitations. To make this a public event, tap the down arrow next to Private Event and select instead Public Event. (On the Facebook website, you select Private or Public when you click the Create Event button.)

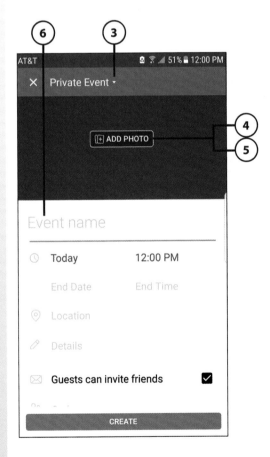

(4) Add a photo for this event by tapping Add Photo (or clicking Upload Photo or Video) and selecting the picture you want to use. (In the mobile app, tap Add Photo and then tap either Upload a New Photo or Choose from Existing Photos.)

(5) To select a visual theme for this website in the mobile app, tap Add Photo and then tap Choose a Theme. On the Facebook website, click Choose a Theme and then make a selection. (You can either choose a theme or use a photo, but you can't do both.)

(6) Enter the name of the event into the Event Name box.

7 Click the Date control (on the website) or tap Today (in the mobile app) and select a date from the pop-up calendar.

8 Click the Time control (on the website) or tap the time (in the mobile app) and select the start time for the event.

9 If you entered a start time, you can also enter an end time for the event. On the website, click the End Time link to display the End section, and then use the controls to set the end date and time. In the mobile app, tap End Date and End Time to set the end date and time.

10 Specify the event's location by entering the location into the Location box.

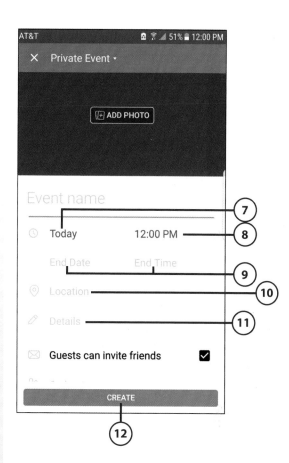

Location

You can enter an exact address as the event's location, a city or state, or even just "My House" or "Room 223 in the Henry Building."

11 Enter any additional details about the event into the Description (website) or Details (mobile app) box.

12 Click the Create or Create Private/ Public Event button to create the event.

Invite Friends to Your Event

Once you've created an event, you need to invite people to attend that event. You do this from the newly created event page.

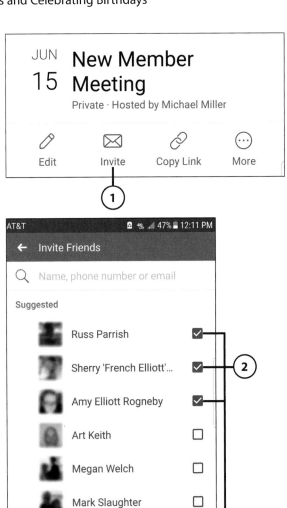

1. From the event page, click or tap Invite to display the Invite pane.

2. Check those friends you want to invite.

3. Click the Send Invites button to send the desired invitations.

Edit or Cancel an Event

It happens. Even the best-laid plans go astray, and you may be forced to change your plans or even cancel a planned event. Here's how you do it.

1. Open the event page and click or tap the Edit button to display the Edit Event panel.

(2) Click or tap to edit any specific piece of information about the event.

(3) Cancel the event by clicking or tapping Cancel Event.

(4) Select Cancel Event to cancel the event but retain all posts and other information pertaining to the event.

(5) Select Delete Event to cancel the event and delete all information about the event.

(6) Enter a message to be sent to anyone scheduled to attend the event.

(7) Click or tap Confirm; all guests will receive a message notifying them that the event is cancelled.

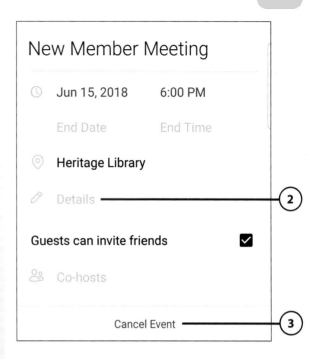

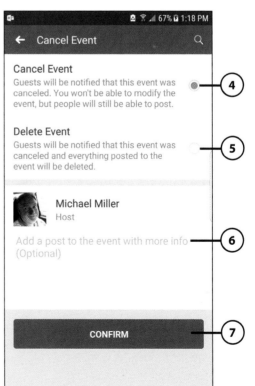

Celebrating Birthdays

Facebook knows a lot about you and your friends, including when you were born. To that end, Facebook does a nice social service by letting you know when someone's birthday is approaching—so that you can send your birthday wishes.

Personal Replies

Most people receive a lot of Facebook greetings on their birthdays. Don't be disappointed if you don't receive a personal thank you from the birthday baby.

View Upcoming Birthdays

Facebook notifies you when it's one of your friends' birthday. You can then leave that person a happy birthday message. It's what people do on Facebook!

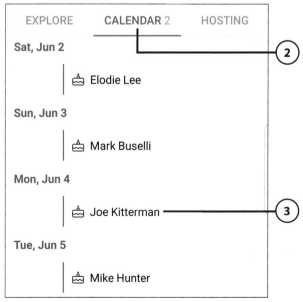

(1) In the mobile app, tap the More icon, and tap Events to display the Events page.

(2) Tap the Calendar tab; then scroll down the timeline to see upcoming birthdays.

(3) Tap a person's name to display his profile page.

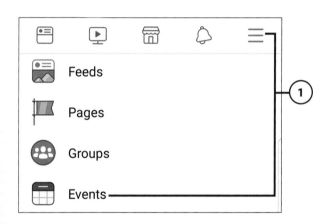

4 Scroll to the Publisher box and write that person a birthday message.

5 On the Facebook website, upcoming birthdays are displayed in the right side of the Home page. (Depending on your notification settings, you may also receive a Facebook notification of the birthday.) Click the name of a person to send that person birthday wishes.

6 Enter your birthday wishes.

7 Click Post.

8 To view all upcoming birthdays on the Facebook website, click Events in the navigation bar to display the Events page.

9 Select Birthdays in the left sidebar.

10 Enter a birthday wish. *Or...*

11 Click the name or picture of the person you want to wish happy birthday. This opens her profile page, where you can enter a birthday wish.

Public Only

Facebook only notifies you of birthdays from friends who have opted to make their birthdays public. Friends with private birthdays do not appear in the birthday list.

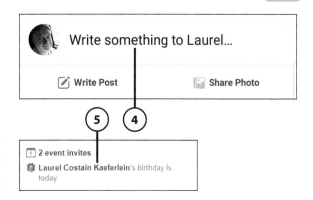

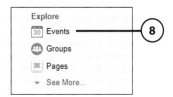

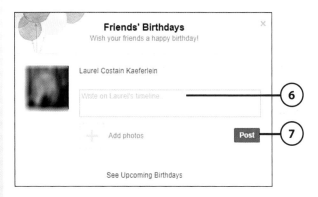

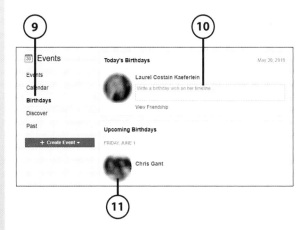

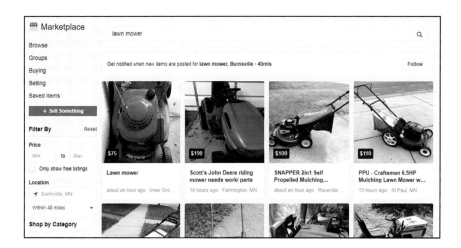

In this chapter, you find out how to buy items from and sell items to other Facebook members via the Facebook Marketplace

→ Shopping for Items in the Facebook Marketplace
→ Selling Your Items in the Facebook Marketplace

Buying and Selling in the Facebook Marketplace

People have been buying and selling online for several decades now, through sites like eBay and Craigslist. Well, Facebook decided that it had what it takes to offer a vibrant online marketplace for its users, so now you have another place to buy and sell stuff online—in the Facebook Marketplace.

The Facebook Marketplace is more like Craigslist than it is eBay. It's basically an online classified ads site to buy and sell items locally. You work out all the details with the buyer or the seller; Facebook doesn't offer payment or shipping services. Find something you like, contact the buyer, and then pay the buyer directly when you pick it up. Same thing with selling; post an item for sale, interested buyers contact you, and then the buyer pays you when he picks it up.

It's as easy as that.

Shopping for Items in the Facebook Marketplace

Facebook supposes (and supposes mostly correctly) that you're more comfortable buying things from friends and friends of friends and other people who use Facebook every day. So the Facebook Marketplace is full of items for sale in your area, that you can easily travel to and purchase. The people listing these items for sale are other Facebook members—sometimes people on your friends' list!

You can browse the listings in the Facebook Marketplace by category or search for specific items. You can even adjust the results to focus on a particular area or location—or change the location to look for items in another city, if you want.

When you find an item you want to buy, simply send a private message to the seller. You can then work out the details on how you want to pay and how best to pick up the item. You pay the seller directly (typically in cash); there's no middleman or third party (like PayPal) involved.

Find an Item to Buy

There are lots of items listed for sale in the Facebook Marketplace. Obviously, you'll see more items listed if you live in a bigger city, but even smaller towns have lots of Facebook members listing items for sale.

Finding the item(s) you want is similar whether you're using the Facebook mobile app or website. We'll focus on the mobile version of Marketplace, but the steps are similar if you're browsing Marketplace on your computer.

1. In the Facebook app, tap the Marketplace icon to open the Marketplace screen.

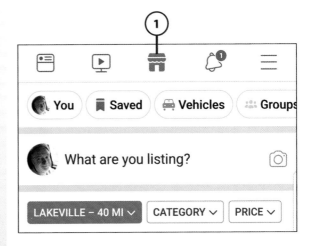

2 Tap one of the buttons at the top of the screen to see items listed for sale in that category.

3 Tap the change location button to change the location for your shopping.

Marketplace on the Web
On the Facebook website, all category, location, and price filters are in the left column.

4 Drag the map to choose your location.

5 Drag the slider to change the distance from your location to search.

6 To change to a more distant location, enter it into the Search by City, Neighborhood, or ZIP Code box.

7 Tap Apply to apply this new location.

8 Tap Category to shop within a specific category.

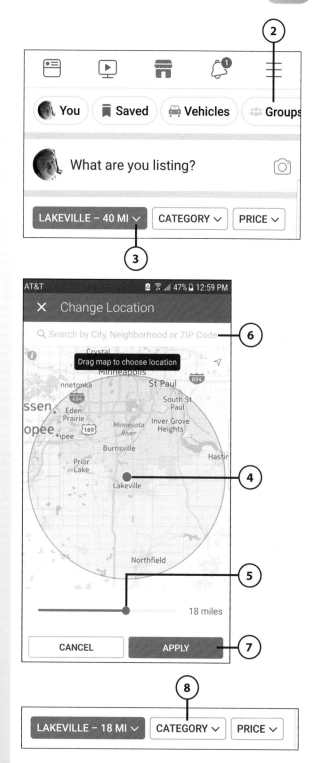

9 Check a category to shop.

10 Tap Apply.

11 Tap Price to limit your shopping to a specific price range.

12 Adjust either end of the slider to narrow your desired price range.

13 Tap Apply.

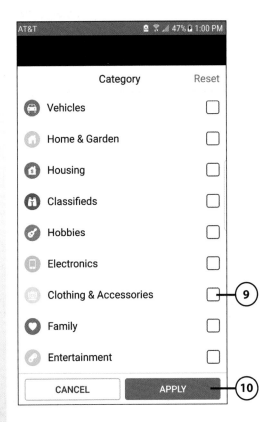

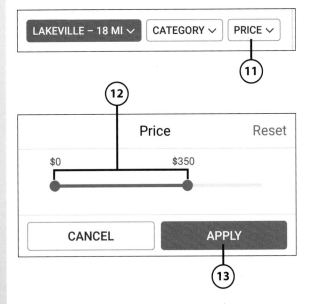

(14) Scroll down to view items for sale. *Or…*

(15) Enter a description of what you're looking for into the Search Marketplace box at the top of the page.

(16) Tap an item to view its full listing.

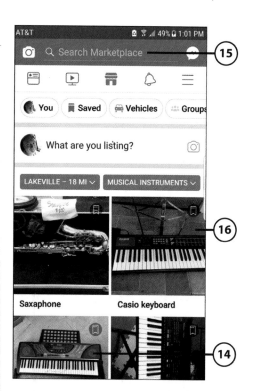

What's for Sale?

People buy and sell all types of items in the Facebook Marketplace. You can find clothing, appliances, electronics, toys, lawn mowers, snow blowers, home and garden items, musical instruments— even cars, boats, and real estate. If you don't see a category for something, search for it instead!

Purchase an Item

Once you've found an item in which you're interested, you can contact the seller to ask questions and arrange a purchase.

(1) Open the listing. You see a picture of the item (if the seller has posted one), the item(s) for sale, and the price. Scroll down to view information about the item(s).

(2) Tap Save to save this item for your future reference.

(3) Tap Share to share this listing with other Facebook friends or post to your News Feed.

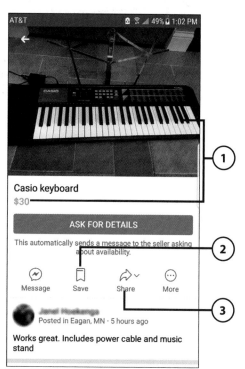

(4) Tap More to report this item or this seller to Facebook. (Use this option if you think there's an issue with the item or if you have a problem with the seller.)

(5) If you have a question about this item or are interested in buying it, tap Ask for Details. An automated message will be sent to the seller, who will respond via Facebook Messenger. You can then ask any questions you have about the item, or arrange to buy it.

(6) It's up to you and the seller to work out the details of the purchase. You can negotiate a lower price (if the seller's willing to bargain), and set a time and place for you to examine and possibly pay for the item. Most Marketplace sales are in cash (few individuals take credit cards or checks), so come prepared to make your purchase!

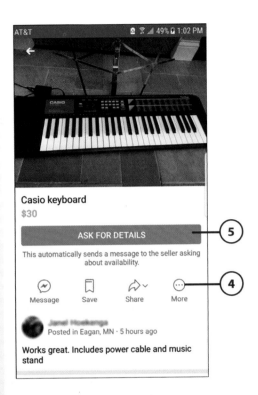

>>>Go Further

SHOP SMART AND SAFE

As with other online marketplaces, such as Craigslist (which is the most similar), you need to take care to ensure your safety when shopping in the Facebook Marketplace. Facebook itself offers no guarantees or protections for items sold via its Marketplace; you're buying directly from an individual seller, not from Facebook, so the transaction is between you and the seller. Facebook only hosts the listings, nothing more.

This means you definitely want to examine an item before you buy; you never want to buy blind. You also want to buy local (which is what the Marketplace is all about); the risks go up exponentially if you buy something sight unseen from someone in a distant location and have the item shipped to you.

When you arrange to look at and perhaps purchase an item, do so at a location where you feel safe. If you go to the seller's house, take someone else with you, just in case. Even better, arrange to meet at a neutral location, if you can, like a coffeeshop or supermarket parking lot.

You'll probably be paying in cash, so have the money in hand and be careful with it. If something seems suspicious or makes you uncomfortable, just walk away.

In any instance, examine the item carefully, because all sales are final. While a seller *could* offer you a refund if you're dissatisfied, most don't, so don't expect it. Look at the item, try it on if that makes sense, and then decide if you want to buy it. (And remember: You can always offer the seller a little less than asking price. As with all types of classified advertising, price is often negotiable.)

Once the purchase is completed, you're done. If the item doesn't work or breaks or whatever, that's now your problem; the seller is not obligated to give you your money back, no matter how high (or low) the purchase price. Hopefully you got a good deal on something you wanted—that's how the Facebook Marketplace is supposed to work.

Selling Your Items in the Facebook Marketplace

It's easy to list an item in the Facebook Marketplace; it's pretty much the same as placing a classified ad in your local paper or posting a listing on Craigslist.

List an Item for Sale

Before you list an item for sale, gather all the details about the product that a buyer might want to know. Also take one or more pictures of your item. (If you're listing from your mobile phone, just take the photos with your phone; you can then add them to your listing from your phone's photo gallery.)

Listing an item is similar in the mobile app and on the Facebook website. We'll describe the app version here.

1. From the main Marketplace page, tap within the What Are You Listing? box. (On the Facebook website, click the Sell Something button.)

2. If you're selling a general item, tap Items for Sale. (Otherwise, tap Vehicles for Sale, Housing for Rent/Sale, or, if you're posting a job listing, Jobs.)

3. Tap Add Photos to add one or more photos of your item. This opens your phone's photo gallery.

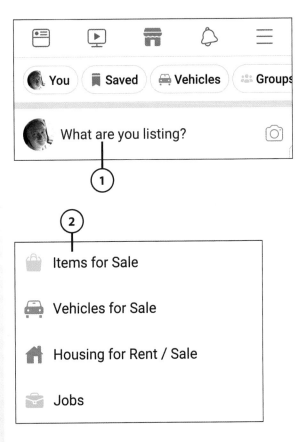

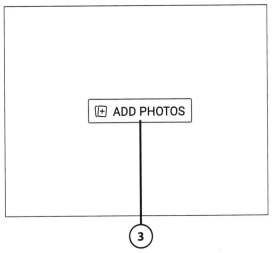

4 Tap the picture(s) you want to display of your item.

5 Tap Next to return to the listing screen.

6 Tap within the What Are You Selling? field and enter the title for your item listing.

7 Tap within the Price field and enter the selling price for your item.

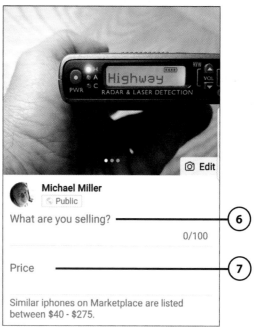

8. Tap within the Category field and select the appropriate category for your item.

9. If necessary, tap within the Location field to change your location.

10. Tap within the Description field and enter a description of your item. The more detailed the description, the better.

11. If you want to ship this item to buyers outside your area, tap "on" the Offer Shipping for This Item switch.

12. Tap Next.

13. Tap where you want this listing displayed—Marketplace (by default) and/or Your Profile.

14. If you belong to a group that might be interested in this item (and that permits for sale listings), tap to select that group.

15. Tap Post, and the item listing is posted.

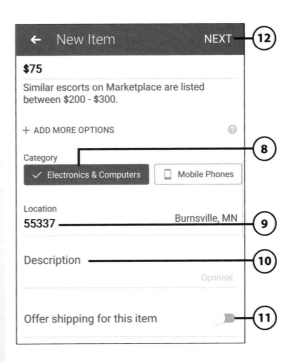

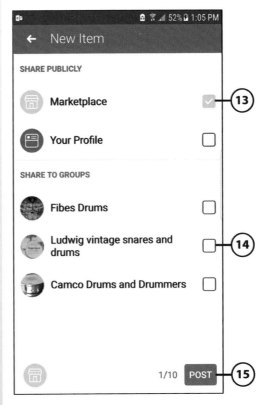

It's Not All Good

Prohibited Items

You can sell just about anything on the Facebook Marketplace, except for the following:

- Adult products or services
- Alcohol
- Ammunition, explosives, and weapons
- Animals
- Digital media
- Healthcare products
- Home services
- Illegal, prescription, and recreational drugs
- Real money gambling services
- Real, virtual, or fake currency
- Subscriptions or digital products
- Tickets to events
- Tobacco products and related paraphernalia
- Unsafe supplements

In addition, item listings cannot be deceptive, fraudulent, misleading, or offensive. You also can't list items that infringe upon or violate the copyright or trademark of any third party.

For more details on what you can and can't sell on the Facebook Marketplace, go to www.facebook.com/policies/commerce.

Manage Your Sale Items

You can keep track of all items currently and previously listed for sale in the Marketplace's Your Items section. This section is also where you can mark an item as sold or remove it from sale.

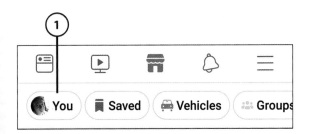

1. In the mobile app, open the main Marketplace page and tap the You button. (On the website, click Selling in the left sidebar.)

2. You now see items you have for sale and those you've previously sold. To view a listing, click or tap it.

3. If you want to edit an item, tap the More button, and then tap Edit Item Details.

4. If you've sold an item, tap Mark as Sold.

5. If you want to delete a listing, tap the More button, and then tap Delete Item.

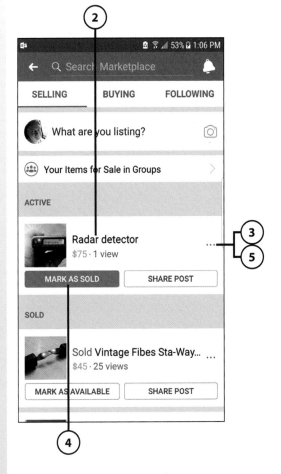

Sell an Item

When someone is interested in your item, you'll receive a private message (in the Messenger app if you have a mobile device). The message will typically be an automated "Is this available?"

Respond to the message to communicate with the interested buyer. Answer any additional questions the person may have.

If the person wants to buy the item, arrange a time and place to meet. The person can come to your home; if so, make sure somebody else is there with you, for safety purposes. (It's often safer to meet at a public place, such as a local business or a school parking lot.)

The buyer may offer to pay a lower price. You can accept this if you want, stick to your original price, or settle somewhere in the middle. That's all part of the negotiation process.

Once the buyer pays you (in cash, probably), you hand over the item, and the transaction is completed. You can then return to the Facebook Marketplace screen in the mobile app or website and mark the item as sold. (Tap You in the app or click Selling on the website, then click or tap Mark as Sold for that item.)

And now you're done!

Cash Is Good

You should probably accept cash payment for the purchase. As for other forms of payment, you likely don't have a credit card terminal, so that's out. If you're comfortable with the technology, you could accept PayPal or Google Pay via a phone app, but that's a lot more complicated. And taking a personal check as payment is just plain risky; you have no idea whether that person has sufficient funds in his checking account. Money orders and cashiers' checks are safe but more trouble for the buyer; they're good for bigger ticket items. For most things you sell, cash is the way to go.

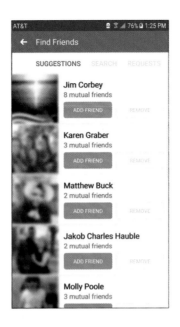

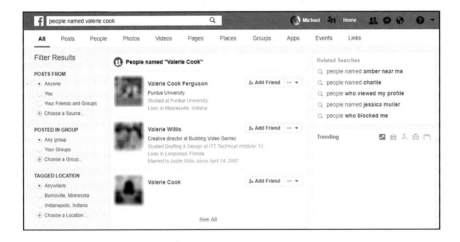

Tips for Communicating with Your Kids and Grandkids on Facebook

Facebook is very popular among middle-aged and older users today, but it started out as a social network for college students. While the current generation of college students has moved onto newer, hipper social media for their own personal use, most younger users still maintain a presence on Facebook—primarily to keep in touch with the older members of their families.

Are Kids Still Using Facebook?

Facebook might be new to you, but it's old news for most younger users. In fact, Facebook used to be the place where all the cool kids hung out. Today, Facebook's user base has shifted toward the older side, and younger users are either using Facebook less or abandoning it completely.

Let's face it—if you're a kid, you don't want to do much of anything that your parents and grandparents are also doing. A website or social network just isn't cool if all the older people you know are using it, too.

And older users definitely are using Facebook. The fastest growing age group on Facebook today is users aged 55 and up, whereas users 35 and up now represent almost half of Facebook's user base. This means that kids in their teens and twenties make up less than half of all Facebook users—even though they used to rule the roost.

This demographic shift is due in part to more older people joining, but also to equally large numbers of younger users leaving. In 2018, the number of Facebook users aged 12 to 24 are expected to decline by almost 6 percent. That's a loss of approximately 2 million younger users.

Whether Facebook likes it or not, the social network is definitely becoming a hangout for older users.

Before this shift, Facebook used to be a good place for parents and grandparents to connect with their kids and grandkids. That's less true today, although there's still a place for Facebook in the intergenerational communication chain.

Even though a lot of younger users are leaving Facebook for good, even more are remaining on Facebook but just using it less. Instead of checking in constantly throughout the day, today's younger generation of Facebook users are more likely to check in just once a day, or maybe once every few days.

In other words, your school-age grandkids and their friends are maintaining their ties to the Facebook community, even as they explore new social networking opportunities elsewhere. Why stay on Facebook if it's no longer cool? Simple: To stay in touch with those non-cool older family members.

That's right—younger users recognize Facebook's valuable role in connecting all family members—younger and older. Your kids, grandkids, and nephews and nieces are staying on Facebook *because* you're there—not in spite of it. They know that you use Facebook to share family news and photos, and there's value in that. It's easier for them to keep up with what's going on by checking in on Facebook every few days. The younger generation might not be using Facebook to talk to one another as much anymore, but they're using it to talk to you and other people who are important to them.

Knowing this changes the way you might have otherwise used Facebook to connect with your grandkids. You no longer have to sneak around the dark corners of Facebook to keep tabs on what the kids are doing; instead, they expect you to be right up front with your comments and pictures and such.

How to Connect with Younger Users on Facebook

If you're in your fifties and sixties (or older), your thirty-something and forty-something children are likely long-time Facebook users. They know how to use Facebook to share and connect with friends and family, and expect you to either do the same or learn how. You'll find them checking their Facebook feeds several times a day.

Your teenage and twenty-something children and grandchildren are also expert in using Facebook, but they use it a whole lot less. They check their News Feeds no more than a few times each week, primarily to see what their parents and other family members are up to. Some still use Facebook to keep in touch with distant friends, although this is becoming less common. Like their parents, these kids are savvy Facebook users, even if they're not on all the time.

Knowing this, you need to connect with your children and grandchildren at a similar level of expertise. You need to know not only how to connect via Facebook, but also what is best to share in that environment. Let's walk through what you need to do.

Make Friends with Your Kids and Grandkids

The first step in using Facebook to connect with your younger family members is to add them to your friends list. It shouldn't be too hard to find your children, grandchildren, nieces, and nephews on Facebook and then send out the necessary friend requests. When your family members are on your friends list, the posts they make should show up in your News Feed.

It's Not All Good

Selected Posts

By default, your kids' and grandkids' posts are visible to all their Facebook friends, including you. More tech-savvy youngsters, however, might figure out how to fine-tune their privacy settings and exclude you (and other family members) from some or all of their posts. This means you *don't* see everything they post in your News Feed. There's no way around this.

(1) Facebook might suggest your family members as friends when you first sign up, when you click the Friend Requests button on the website's toolbar, or when you tap the Notifications icon in the mobile app—especially if you have their addresses in your email contacts list. If so, click the Add Friend button.

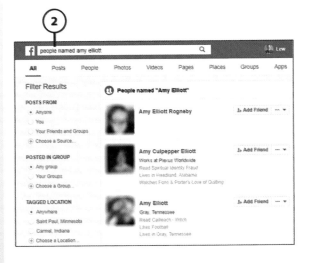

Finding Friends

Learn how to find family and friends on Facebook in Chapter 3, "Finding Friends on Facebook."

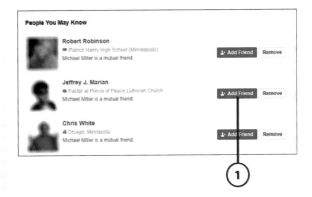

(2) Alternatively, you can do a simple search for your kids and grandkids. Use the search box in the Facebook toolbar or the top of the Facebook app to search for **people named *john doe*** and your family member's name should pop up. (In this and other examples, replace "john doe" with the name of the person you're searching for.)

Put Your Family Members in a Special Friends List

Just as you can read your kids' and grandkids' posts on Facebook, they can also read your status updates in their News Feeds. However, your grandkids might not be interested in everything you post, especially those posts that deal with issues of interest to you and your friends.

The solution is to not send all your posts to the youngsters. Instead, you can create a *friends list* that contains only selected family members. You can then opt to hide your posts from members of that list—or send selected posts only to your family members. It's an easy way to deal with groups of people (in this instance, your family members) with a single click.

It's Not All Good

They Love You, But...

Depending on what you post on Facebook, your kids and grandkids might find your status updates charming. Or they might find them embarrassing or even totally uninteresting. Let's face it: The kinds of things that interest someone our age aren't likely to be engrossing to the average teenager. For that matter, all those words of wisdom and inspiration that you like to post are likely to be roundly ignored by youngsters with more immediate things on their minds.

In other words, don't expect the younger generations to like and comment on everything you post. At best, they might read your posts and then move on. At worst, they might figure out how to block your posts—or even unfriend you.

(1) Start by creating a new Facebook friends list that contains all your children and grandchildren. On the Facebook website, go to the profile page for your first family member, click the Friends button, and then click Add to Another List.

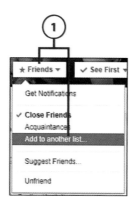

(2) Facebook creates a number of "smart" lists, based on personal information you've added to your account. One of these smart lists, named Family, is just for your family members. Click Family to add this person to your Family list. Repeat these two steps for each of your family members.

(3) Now you can configure your privacy settings so that your family members don't see the bulk of your posts. Start a new post as normal, and then tap or click the privacy button.

(4) Click or tap Friends Except.

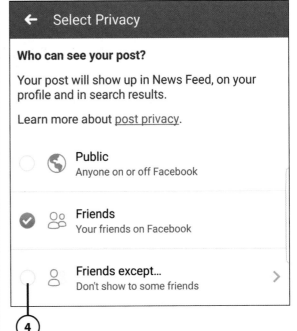

5 Scroll down to the Friend Lists section, and then click or tap Family and complete the post as normal. This and all subsequent posts (until you change the privacy setting) will now be visible to everyone *except* your family members.

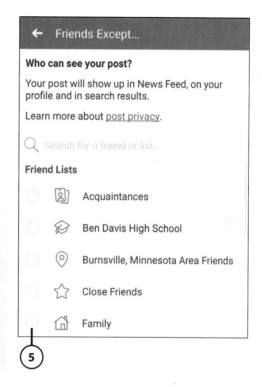

Privacy Settings

Learn about Facebook's privacy settings in Chapter 9, "Managing Your Privacy on Facebook."

Share Photos and Videos

Just as you can read each other's status updates, you can also share photos and videos with your children and grandchildren.

To this end, you should encourage your grandkids or their parents to post photos and videos of themselves to Facebook. This provides you a constantly updated photo album of your loved ones.

You should also try to post the occasional photo or video of yourself, for your family members to see. Don't limit yourself to posed pictures, either; your younger grandkids especially will get a big kick out of any crazy or silly picture or video you upload.

Pictures and Movies

Learn more about sharing photos and videos in Chapter 10, "Viewing and Sharing Photos and Videos."

Chat via Text and Video

If you're on one side of the country and your kids and grandkids are on the other, or even if you're only a few states away, you might only see your family in person one or two times a year. With Facebook text and video chat, you can visit with each other several times a week, if you like. It can truly bring together distant families.

Chatting is easier if everybody expects it. To this end, try to schedule time for a weekly video chat with each of your children and grandchildren. This is especially great for talking to your younger grandkids who are sure to appreciate the one-on-one time with their favorite grandpa or grandma.

For the teenagers in your family, Facebook's text chat might be more up their alley. Chatting on Facebook is just like texting on a mobile phone, and you know your kids and grandkids are okay with that. Next time you're on Facebook, check to see if your favorite grandchild is also online and, if so, open a text chat and say hi. If she wants to turn it into a video chat, you always have that option.

Facebook Chat

Learn more about text and video chatting in Chapter 12, "Chatting with Facebook Messenger."

Play Games Together

Here's one you might not have thought of. If your grandkids are like mine, they love to play games—board games, card games, video games, you name it. Well, Facebook is chock full of social games that you can play with other Facebook users. That means all you have to do is pick a game and then invite your grand-kids (or even your grown children) to play it with you, online.

What games are good to play with the younger members of your family? Board games are good, as are card games, word games, and trivia games. Just go to the Games Center page—on the Facebook website, expand the Explore section in the navigation sidebar, and then click Games; in the Facebook app, tap the More icon, tap See More, and then tap Games. From there you can browse or search for games by name or type.

Five Things *Not* to Do with Your Kids and Grandkids on Facebook

If your children and grandchildren are still on Facebook, you need to make sure you don't drive them away with inappropriate (for them) behavior. With that in mind, here are some important things *not* to do when posting and responding to your kids and grandkids.

1. Don't friend their friends. Your kids and grandkids like to keep their friends and family separate, so a family member getting friendly with one of their peers is a big social no-no. Resist the urge to send a friend request to one of your children's or grandchildren's Facebook friends. It's okay for you to accept a friend request if one of her friends invites you, but it's not okay for you to initiate the contact. In general, you should keep your circle of friends to your friends and immediate family, not to your grandchildren's friends.

2. Don't post unflattering photos of them. Family photos that you think are funny might not seem so funny to your kids or grandkids—especially when their friends see them. The problem comes if you upload an embarrassing photo to Facebook and tag a relative in it. Thus tagged, all her Facebook friends will see the photo, with the resulting mortification. Think twice before you post those "cute" photos, especially as they get older. And if you must post the photos, don't tag them by name. If they're not tagged, their friends probably won't see the photos—which is best for all concerned.

3. Don't use their photo as your profile picture. I know you're really proud of your grandkids, but you shouldn't appropriate their photos as your own. Many grandparents use photos of their grandkids as their own profile pictures, or as their pages' cover images. That's not fair to your grandkids—and, to be fair, it looks kind of weird. Post your own photo as your profile picture, and be done with it.

4. Don't post too much personal information. Facebook is a great forum for keeping friends and family up-to-date on what's happening in your life, but that doesn't mean you need to post every little detail about what's happening. Your kids and grandkids, especially, will be embarrassed or even grossed out if you post all the fiddly details about your latest medical exam or (God forbid) romantic interlude. There's just some stuff that kids don't want to know, and you need to know that. (In addition, you want to keep your younger grandkids as safe as possible online, which also argues for sharing as little personal information as possible.)

5. Don't try to be cool. I know, you want to fit in with the young generation today, but let's face it—you're not that young, and you're not that cool. Don't embarrass yourself by trying to use today's hip lingo, or even common Facebook abbreviations, such as LOL (laughing out loud). No matter how hip you think you might be, you'll still come off as an old fogey trying to act younger than you really are. Bottom line: When you're posting on Facebook, act your age. You've earned the privilege.

>>>Go Further

OTHER PLACES TO FIND YOUR KIDS AND GRANDKIDS ONLINE

So if all the hip young kids are leaving Facebook (or using it a lot less on a regular basis), where are they going? There's no one destination for your grandkids and their friends; the younger generation is splintering their time between a number of social media startups. Here are some of the more popular social media used by pre-teens, teens, and twenty-somethings today:

- **Instagram** (www.instagram.com), a social network that lets users shoot and share photos and short videos from their mobile phones.
- **Snapchat** (www.snapchat.com), an image-based smartphone messaging app that erases all posts after they've been viewed.
- **Twitter** (www.twitter.com), a kind of cross between an instant messaging service and a full-blown social network; users post short (280-character max) text messages and photos, called *tweets*, that are then broadcast publicly to that person's followers on the service.

These three social networks are popular among teens and millennials. If you know your kids and grandkids are big on Instagram or Snapchat and you want to stay in touch, you might want to investigate.

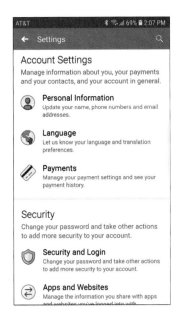

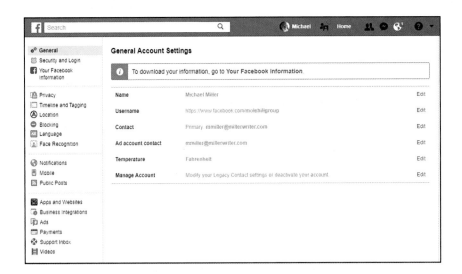

In this chapter, you learn how to configure various aspects of your Facebook account.

→ Changing Your Account Settings
→ Leaving Facebook
→ Dealing with Death

18

Managing Your Facebook Account—Even When You're Gone

Your Facebook account contains your basic personal information—your name, email address, password, and the like. What do you do if you move, get a new email account, or find that your password is compromised? Fortunately, Facebook lets you easily change any and all of this information, at any time.

Changing Your Account Settings

You can change all your Facebook settings from the Account Settings page on either the Facebook website or the mobile app.

Access Account Settings on the Facebook Website

If you're using Facebook on your notebook or desktop computer, you access the Account Settings page from the Facebook toolbar. Once you display the Account Settings page, you click a specific tab to view and edit that type of information.

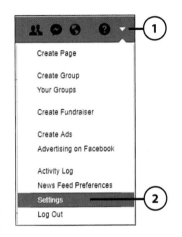

(1) Click the down arrow on the far right of the Facebook toolbar to display the menu of options.

(2) Click Settings to display the Account Settings page.

(3) Click the desired tab on the left to edit that type of information.

Access Account Settings in the Facebook Mobile App

If you're using Facebook on your smartphone or tablet, you access the Account Settings page from the More menu. Once you display the Account Settings page, you tap a specific option to view and edit that type of information.

(Here's how it looks on an Android phone; the steps are similar on an iPhone or iPad.)

1) Tap More.

2) Scroll down and tap to expand the Settings & Privacy section.

3) Tap Account Settings.

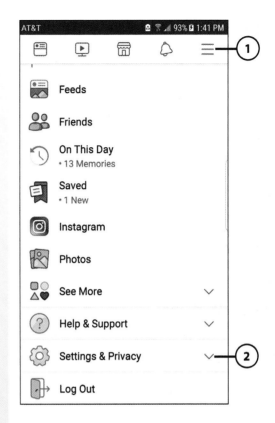

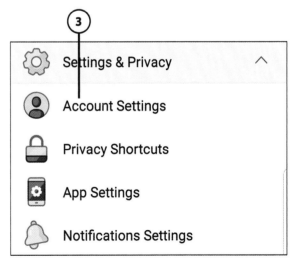

Leaving Facebook

If you ever choose to leave Facebook, you have two options. You can *deactivate* your account, which temporarily hides your account information from others, or you can *delete* your account, which permanently removes your account information.

Deactivate Your Account

Deactivating your account is meant as a temporary solution that you can undo at any future point. When you deactivate your account, Facebook doesn't actually delete your account information; it merely hides it so others can't view it. Because your account information still exists, it's simple enough to reactivate a deactivated account.

You can deactivate your account from either the Facebook website or the mobile app:

- From the website, open the Settings page and then select General, Manage Your Account, Deactivate Your Account.

- In the mobile app, tap More, Settings & Privacy, Settings, Personal Information, Manage Account, Deactivate.

Enter your Facebook password when prompted; then select Continue. On the next page, Facebook gives you several reasons to stay. You can ignore these. Instead, scroll to the Reason for Leaving section and select why it is you're leaving. This is a requirement; you have to tell Facebook something here. Then click or tap the Deactivate button, and your account is deactivated.

Permanently Delete Your Facebook Account

If you're absolutely, positively sure you'll never want to be a Facebook user again—and you want more reassurance that your personal data has been wiped—then you want to permanently delete your account. This is more difficult to do than deactivating your account for the simple reason that your Facebook account is likely connected to lots of other websites.

The first thing you need to do is to go to each website you've linked to your Facebook account and disconnect the link—that is, create a new login ID that is not related to your Facebook ID. Do *not* log into these sites with your Facebook account!

Then you can follow these steps on the Facebook website.

It's Not All Good

It's Final

Deleting your Facebook account is final; all your status updates and other information will be permanently erased. If you later want to rejoin Facebook, you'll have to start completely from scratch.

As with account deactivation, you can delete your account from either the Facebook website or the mobile app:

- On the Facebook website, log in to your account and go to Facebook's Delete My Account page (www.facebook.com/help/delete_account). You have to enter this URL directly into your web browser; there's no link to this page from the Facebook website.

- In the mobile app, select More, Settings & Privacy, Settings, Delete Your Account and Information.

Enter your password, if prompted, and then follow the onscreen instructions to permanently delete your account.

It's Not All Good

14 Days

When you follow this procedure, Facebook deletes your account—so long as you don't log back in to Facebook or log onto any websites that you log into with your Facebook account for the next 14 days. Any interaction with your Facebook account during this 14-day period reactivates your account. This also means not clicking the Facebook Like button on any other website.

Dealing with Death

Here's a question none of us want to face but all of us will have to: What happens to your Facebook account when you die?

The legal status of one's online accounts is a growing issue as online users age. After all, only you are supposed to have access to your online accounts; only you know your password to get into Facebook, Twitter, or even your online banking site (although you could share these with a loved one, for security purposes). And if you aren't able to get online, because you're dead, how can your accounts be put on hold or deleted?

Facebook, fortunately, has considered this situation and offers several options for accounts belonging to deceased members: You can memorialize the account, or you can simply remove it from the Facebook site.

Memorialize an Account

If you choose to memorialize the deceased's account, Facebook retains that person's profile page but locks it so that no one can log into it and so no new friends can be accepted. Current friends, however, can share memories of the deceased on the memorialized timeline, and all existing content remains available for friends to view. (Who can view it depends on the Timeline's existing privacy settings.)

Anyone can report a deceased user to Facebook and thus begin the memorialization process. From your web browser, go to www.facebook.com/help/contact/234739086860192 to display Facebook's Memorialization Request page. Enter the requested information (including information about the person's death), and let Facebook do the rest.

It's Not All Good

Mistaken Memorialization

What do you do if someone memorializes your account—either on purpose or by mistake—and you're not dead yet? You need to contact Facebook via a special form to say you're still alive and want to continue using your account. You won't be able to log into Facebook if your account is in a memorialized state, so go to www.facebook.com/help/contact/292558237463098 and fill out the form there.

Name a Legacy Contact

You can prepare for the inevitable (and make things easier for your surviving friends and family) by designating someone to manage your Facebook account after your passing. This person will be your account's legacy contact and can handle all the details involved with memorializing your account.

You can do this from either the Facebook website or the mobile app:

- On the Facebook website, go to the Settings page; then select General, Manage Account.

- In the mobile app, select More, Settings & Privacy, Settings, Personal Information, Manage Account, Legacy Contact.

From here, follow the onscreen instructions to choose a friend to be your legacy contact.

Remove an Account

If you'd rather not have a loved one's Facebook account memorialized, you can ask Facebook to remove the person's account from the site. This is also an option if a loved one is medically incapacitated.

From your web browser, go to www.facebook.com/help/contact/228813257197480 to display the Special Request for Medically Incapacitated or Deceased Person's Account page. Enter the deceased's name, the URL of his Facebook profile page, and his email address (if you know it); then follow the onscreen instructions to complete the process.

Downloading Content from a Deceased Person's Account

If you've been named as a legacy contact by a loved one before this person passed away, Facebook will contact you with instructions on how to download all that person's Facebook data. If your loved one didn't name a legacy contact, a family member or close friend can retrieve that person's data after death, but with some effort; you'll need a scan of the deceased's driver's license or other government-issued ID, as well as a copy of the death certificate. You can then go to www.facebook.com/help/contact/398036060275245 to display Requesting Content from a Deceased Person's Account page, and follow the instructions there.

Glossary

Activity Log   A chronological list of all your activity on the Facebook site, including status updates, comments on others' posts, and more.

album   A collection of photos or videos uploaded to Facebook.

bot   An automated software program designed to create and control a fake Facebook account.

chat   Private messaging between two or more users.

Chat bar   Click to display a list of Facebook friends who are currently online and available for chatting.

chat heads   Visual representation of people you're chatting with that float above other apps on your mobile device. Available on Facebook's Android app.

Check In   A feature of Facebook that lets you identify your current location.

clickbait   A post or article that attempts to "bait" you into clicking to learn more.

Comment   Your personal reply to a Facebook post.

cover image   The large "banner" photograph that displays across the top of your profile page.

emoji   A small image or icon that conveys an emotion or idea.

event   A Facebook page devoted to a particular online or real-world occasion. You can invite your Facebook friends to events you create.

Facebook   The world's largest social network, with more than one billion users.

Facebook Live   A real-time video broadcast to other Facebook users.

Facebook Marketplace   A forum of classified ads for buying from and selling to other local Facebook users.

Facebook Messenger   Facebook's mobile app for public and private messaging.

Facebook toolbar   The collection of clickable icons that appears at the top of every Facebook page.

fake news   In the strictest sense, deliberately fictional news presented as real news. Some politicians refer to any legitimate reporting they don't like as "fake news," thus diluting the impact of the term.

friend   On Facebook, a user with whom you share posts. Users have to agree to join your friends list by accepting a friend request.

friend request   An invitation to join a user's friends list.

Group   A Facebook page devoted to a specific topic or community of users.

hashtag   A word or phrase that starts with the hash (#) character and describes the content of your post—and that readers can click to see similar posts with the same hashtag.

Instagram   A social network that lets users share photos and short videos from their mobile phones.

legacy contact   A friend or family member designated to manage your Facebook account after your death.

lightbox   A photo-viewing window superimposed over the normal News Feed.

Like   Giving a virtual "thumbs up" if you approve of a Facebook post—or, in the case of company or celebrity Pages, a way to follow posts from that entity.

link   A clickable link to a web page outside the Facebook site.

meme   A concept or catchphrase or image that spreads in a viral fashion over the Internet.

Messages   Facebook's private messaging system.

mobile app   A software application for smartphone or tablet. Facebook offers several mobile apps for users.

mobile website   The version of the Facebook website that displays when you access facebook.com from a mobile device.

Most Recent   A view of the Facebook News Feed that displays the most recent posts from your friends.

navigation sidebar   The list of links to various pages and services found on the left side of the Facebook website.

News Feed   A stream of status updates from a user's friends.

notification   A message or alert from Facebook.

On This Day   A new Facebook post that includes one or more posts from this same day in the past.

Page   A Facebook page for a celebrity, company, or other public figure or entity.

post   See *status update*.

Privacy button   Click to determine who can see a given post or piece of information.

profile picture   The picture (typically of you) that displays on your Timeline page and accompanies all posts you make on the Facebook site.

Public   The privacy setting that enables anyone on Facebook to see a given post or piece of information.

Publisher box   Where you enter the text for a new status update.

share   On the Facebook site, reposting someone else's status update to your friends list.

Snapchat   An image-based smartphone messaging app that erases all posts after they've been viewed.

social game   A game you play online either against other Facebook users or by sharing information with other Facebook users.

social media   See *social network.*

social network   An Internet-based service that hosts a community of users and makes it easy for those users to communicate with one another.

status update   A short message (with text and/or images and video) that updates friends on what a user is doing or thinking.

tag   Identifying a friend in a post or a photo.

Timeline   That part of a user's profile page that displays past status updates in reverse chronological order.

Top Stories   A view of the Facebook News Feed that displays the most important posts from your friends.

Trending   A section on the Facebook home page that displays the most currently active or interesting topics.

Twitter   A cross between an instant messaging service and a full-blown social network; users post short (280-character max) text messages and images, called *tweets*, that are then broadcast publicly to that person's followers on the service.

unfriend   The process of removing a person from your Facebook friends list.

URL   Uniform Resource Locator; the address of a web page.

video chat   A face-to-face onscreen chat between two users.

viral   A post, picture, or video that spreads quickly from person to person until thousands of people have seen it.

YouTube   The Internet's largest video sharing community.

Index

via fake accounts, 148
via sharing posts, 149
donations, soliciting, 116-117
down arrow button
    iPad app, 21
    on website, 11
downloading
    content from deceased person's
        account, 287
    photos, 185-186

E

echo chamber, 151
editing
    Activity Log, 63-64
    advertiser-shared data, 169-170
    events, 250-251
    profile page
        on website, 12
        updating personal information,
            58-61
effects, shooting selfies with, 189-191
email addresses
    confirmation message, 7
    creating Facebook accounts, 5
    finding friends, 36
embarrassing photos in posts/status
    updates, 129
emojis, 73
    in status updates, including, 108-109
Employer section on website, 35

etiquette for posts/status updates, 120
    from family members, 277-278
    shorthand (abbreviations), 131-132
    writing posts, 130-131
events, 243
    canceling, 250-251
    editing, 250-251
    finding, 245
    invitations, responding to, 244-245
    scheduling, 247
        creating event, 247-249
        inviting friends, 250
    types of, 247
    viewing, 13, 245-246
Explore section on website, 12

F

Facebook
    accessing, via website versus mobile
        app, 26-27
    accounts
        confirmation message, 7
        creating, 5-6
        deactivating, 284
        deceased users, 286
        deleting, 284-285
        deleting due to death, 287
        downloading content from deceased
            person's account, 287
        fake, 148
        legacy contacts, 287

G

M

O–P

Q–R

V

X–Y–Z

Answers to Your Technology Questions

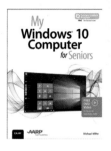

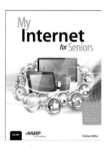

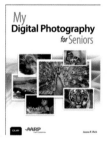

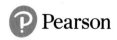

The **My...For Seniors Series** is a collection of how-to guide books from AARP and Que that respect your smarts without assuming you are a techie. Each book in the series features:

- Large, full-color photos
- Step-by-step instructions
- Helpful tips and tricks

For more information about these titles, and for more specialized titles, visit
informit.com/que